THE FIRST AND ONLY

INDIA & THE NORDICS
STORIES ACROSS TWO CONTINENTS

BREAKING BARRIERS, BUILDING FUTURES

A DMI PUBLICATION
EDITED BY **RINA SUNDER**

To Morten B. Mærli,

I hope to be yours in every lifetime to come.

Rina Sunder

Author Bio

Rina Sunder is a leading voice in cross-cultural leadership, gender equality, and India-Nordic collaboration. With a career spanning the public, private, investment, and nonprofit sectors, Sunder has led pioneering initiatives in circular economy, ethical trade, and women's empowerment and is widely recognized for elevating female voices in international discourse. She is the author of the textbook Det Moderne India and is frequently invited to comment on global affairs, diplomacy, and India-Norway relations on both Norwegian and Indian television.

As co-founder of Det Moderne India (DMI), she works at the intersection of policy and business to drive impactful partnerships between the Global North and South. DMI has been supported by the Nordic Council of Ministers and featured at high-level platforms, including the World Economic Forum in Davos.

She also hosts Det Moderne India Podcast and curates dialogues on diversity, geopolitics, and sustainable development.

Rina chose to write *The First and Only: India & The Nordics— Breaking Barriers, Building Futures* because it reflects her own journey. Since the age of 20, Sunder has often found herself as the *"first and only"*—the only woman with an Indian background in her academic cohort, the sole woman in male-dominated professional spaces, and later, as Chair of the Norway India Chamber of Commerce and

Industry, frequently the only woman of color at conferences, seminars, and on panels.

These experiences shaped her understanding of both the visible and invisible barriers women face, especially those navigating multiple identities.

The book is her way of honouring others who have walked similar paths and creating space for more inclusive, cross-cultural leadership.

With Masters degrees from BI Norwegian Business School and Denmark's Copenhagen Business School in Norway and Denmark, Sunder brings a distinct intersectional perspective shaped by her lived experience as a trailblazer. Recognized for her advocacy and thought leadership, she continues to be a powerful voice for inclusive, sustainable, and globally connected progress.

The First and Only: India & The Nordics – Breaking Barriers, Building Futures

Foreword by May-Elin Stener, Ambassador of Norway to India

The First and Only:India & The Nordics – Breaking Barriers, Building Futures

– by Rina Sunder

Almost two years ago, I was presenting my credentials as Norwegian Ambassador to India to the Honorable President, Draupadi Murmu. As I entered the meeting hall with my all-women Norwegian team, she looked at us and exclaimed in Hindi - Nari Shakti - 'women power'.

As the Ambassador of Norway to India, I have for the past two years had the privilege of witnessing the dynamism, resilience, and leadership of Indian women and girls across diverse sectors. From boardrooms to classrooms, and from grassroots' movements to government, their strength is not just admirable - it is transformational.

Gender equality is a global challenge but one that manifests uniquely in India. To further global gender justice, I believe cross-cultural exchange and international cooperation are important. Coming from a Nordic country, where gender equality is a cornerstone of our society, I am very aware that the road to equality is neither short nor simple. It requires intention, persistence, and visibility. The Nordics can also learn a lot from India in our pursuit of sustainable and technological growth. This is what makes this book so timely and vital.

Through the voices of Indian and Nordic women leaders in this book, we are welcomed into insights that are both personal and political. Each story is a window into the reality of navigating leadership as a woman in different cultures and industries.

I believe that storytelling and personal narratives can be very powerful when it comes to shifting mindsets. Thanks to Rina Sunder's thoughtful curation of this book, based on a mix of personal narratives, policy insights, and data-driven analysis, important female voices will now be heard, and structural challenges will be raised.

I hope this book will also inspire new pathways for collaboration between the Nordics and India. We may be oceans apart, but we are united by our shared belief in the power of transformative dialogue and sustainable progress.

To all readers: listen closely. These stories will not only inspire but lead to action; in boardrooms, in communities, and in policy circles.

Introduction

The First and Only: India & The Nordics - Breaking Barriers, Building Futures

The *First and Only* explores how India and the Nordic countries are reshaping their relationship, with a focus on gender equality and common aspirations for a better future. This book shares the inspiring stories of change-makers—women, corporations, and NGOs that are creating new opportunities and men who support them as allies and mentors.

At its core, the *First and Only* refers to those who step into uncharted territory—women, organizations, and leaders who take bold steps where no paths previously existed. They are the pioneers who break glass ceilings, create change, and reshape societies, paving the way where there are no precedents. It could be the first woman to enter a man's profession, the first organization to take the risk of defying gender norms in leadership positions, or the first NGO to advocate for structural change. The journey of a *First and Only* is one of courage, perseverance, and transformation.

The book is structured into multiple sections. Each highlights a critical aspect of Indo-Nordic collaboration and the challenges faced by women.

Part 1: India and the Nordics - an overview

The book begins by exploring the increasingly robust connections between India and the Nordic countries, examining economic collaborations and innovative policies. It then proceeds to examine how both parties utilize technology, renewable energy, and inclusive governance to build sustainable futures before turning to gender equality. We also explore the role of women in Indian culture and the policies that have enabled women in the Nordics to join and thrive in the workforce.

Then we move on to examine the obstacles, cultural disparities, and innovative solutions that influence the inclusion of women in the workforce. Although India has undergone fast economic expansion, extensive gender gaps persist, rooted in social norms, workplace prejudices, and system issues. This section captures the opinions of experts, industry captains, and personal experiences. It discusses how companies, policymakers, and change-makers are trying to close these gaps and provides practical ways to make the workforce more inclusive and equitable.

Part 2: The legacy of breaking barriers

This section goes beyond individual stories to explore the grit, perseverance, resilience and value-driven leadership in the careers of pioneering women. It acknowledges the unseen price of breaking barriers—the emotional vulnerability, personal sacrifices, and the weight of representation that trailblazers must carry.

Throughout history, those who are the *First and Only* have faced resistance—not just from the world around them but also from the invisible burdens that come with pioneering change. The cost of breaking barriers is rarely fully discussed. While society celebrates the trailblazers, their sacrifices, vulnerability, the loneliness of leadership, and the constant pressure to represent and succeed remain largely unseen. This section highlights these realities—demonstrating how resilience and determination shape those who dare to lead.

Part 3: Leading with purpose

This part highlights the remarkable journeys of five outstanding leaders: Anette Holte, Kristin Andresen, Vidya Basarkod, Anna Wagner Norseng, and Ajaita Shah. They achieved great things in their respective fields despite the odds. Their experiences show that resilience, adaptability, and a clear vision are crucial for transformation.

Part 4: Men as allies - supporting women

Here, we'll explore how mentorship, partnership, and allyship can support more women in stepping into leadership. We demonstrate how men—husbands, fathers, business leaders or entrepreneurs—have an essential role in helping women demolish barriers and move into positions of leadership. By sharing personal stories, reflections and specific actions, Part 5 emphasizes how male allies can play a key role in moving toward a more inclusive and equitable future.

Part 5: India's IT Gender Balance - A Model for the Nordics

In this part, we zoom into tech and the future. Surprisingly, India has emerged as a frontrunner in female involvement in the tech sector, with women constituting 35 percent of the IT workforce. This figure is well above that of the Nordic countries, where participation remains lower, even in the face of robust gender equality initiatives. This gap prompts important questions: How has India, with fewer formal gender protections, managed to draw more women into tech than the Nordics?

In this part, we'll dive deeper into both regions to unpack the structural and cultural elements that lead to these differences. We'll also focus on India's corporate-driven inclusion strategies, digital advancements, and specific government efforts. At the same time, it examines how the Nordic model of work-life balance and legal protections offer valuable lessons for sustaining long-term gender equality in tech. By learning from each other, both regions can foster a more inclusive and diverse digital economy.

Final thoughts

This book could not have been made without the support of the Nordic Council of Ministers, whose commitment to gender equality and sustainability has been key to fostering cross-regional dialogue and collaboration.

Most of the cases featured in this book originate from podcast conversations DMI has had with our respective guests. However, in Part 3, where we go beyond the polished and public narratives, we have conducted independent research, with all references sourced from media and online sources.

Through a mix of personal narratives, policy insights, and data-driven analysis, *The First and Only* presents a compelling vision of how India and the Nordics can learn from each other in their pursuit of equality and sustainable growth.

This book is not just a review of history—it is about what lies ahead and how those who are pushing boundaries today are paving the way for a more inclusive future.

13

Contents

Part 1

Part 2

Part 3

Part 4

Part 5

Contents

Part 1

Chapter 1
India and the Nordics - An Overview

The Nordic region

The Nordic region—comprising Norway, Sweden, Denmark, Finland, and Iceland—is widely recognized for its strong economies, innovation, productivity, and comprehensive welfare systems. For more than six decades, the Nordic countries have maintained a shared labour mobility agreement, allowing citizens to work across borders without the requirement of visas.

These Nordic countries have been working together politically for a long time. About 27.8 million people live in the Nordics. The Nordic countries consistently rank among the wealthiest in the world, with high gross domestic product per capita, reflecting strong economic performance and a high standard of living.

There are no huge gaps between the rich and the poor. The average female labour force participation rate in the Nordic countries is approximately 73%.

Nordic men take the most paternity leave in the world. This shows they have policies that help people balance work and family and share responsibilities at home.

This focus on gender equality is reflected in politics too. The Nordics have been electing women to lead for a long time. In 2021 and 2022, Norway, Denmark, Sweden, and Finland all had women as prime ministers. This precedent began in 1980, when Iceland elected Vigdís Finnbogadóttir as the world's first democratically elected female president. She was in office for 16 years, showing everyone that women could lead. In Norway, Gro Harlem Brundtland became the first female prime minister in 1986 and was re-elected in 1990. Erna Solberg, from the Conservative Party, became Norway's second female prime minister in 2013. Finland has also had several female leaders, including Anneli Jäätteenmäki in 2003, Mari Kiviniemi in 2010, and Sanna Marin in 2019. Marin was the youngest head of state in the world when she became Prime Minister in 2019.

The terms "Nordic Region" and "Scandinavia" are frequently conflated, although they refer to different geographic groupings. But Scandinavia is just Denmark, Norway, and Sweden. Even though they are not exactly the same, they work together a lot through the Nordic Council and the Nordic Council of Ministers. Denmark, Sweden, and Finland are in the European Union, but Norway and Iceland are part of the European Economic Area.

Nordic countries consistently rank among the highest globally in metrics such as transparency, public trust, environmental performance, and subjective well-being.

India: A Diverse, Innovative, and Influential Nation

India, with one of the world's fastest-growing economies and the biggest population, is a prominent player on the world stage. India's civilization dates back over 5,000 years, with a longstanding legacy as a center of knowledge, culture, and linguistic diversity.

India is the world's fifth-largest economy based on GDP and the third-largest by how much people can buy. Since opening up its economy in 1991, changes occurred rapidly in the country. As a result of growth in the number of factories, a strong service sector, and the emergence of new businesses, India has become a hub for technology, medicine, and innovation. Additionally, government also invests heavily in renewable energy, with the goal to become a leader in green technology and sustainability.

India has over 500 million workers and a predominantly young population. More than half of the Indian population are under 25, and over 65% are under 35. This group, called generation Z, has about 377 million people, making it the biggest generation ever in India. Although such figures do not guarantee growth, a young and growing population is no doubt, an asset to the country. By 2030, India should have the world's largest working-age population, which should give it a big economic edge and make it a key player in global growth. Yet, problems remain: the low participation of females in the labour force, the disparity of economic development among the regions, and the need to train the labour force to cope with the demands of an expanding economy.

India is active in world affairs. It helped found the United Nations, leads in the Global South, and is a key member of groups like the G20, BRICS, and the World Trade Organization. India pushes for a fairer world order. The country is invested in resolving global issues such as climate change, facilitating peacekeeping, tech deals, and trade talks, especially helping other countries in the Global South. India is actively combating climate change and promoting global sustainability through initiatives like the International Solar Alliance (ISA), which aims to mobilize over $1 trillion in investments by 2030. Additionally, India has set ambitious renewable energy targets, aiming for 450 GW of renewable energy capacity by 2030.

Education and research have always been important in India. India is home to some of the oldest universities, like Nalanda and Takshashila. Today, India is ranked high in the fields of science, technology, and medicine, producing top engineers, doctors, and business people. Schools like the Indian Institutes of Technology (IITs) and Indian Institutes of Management (IIMs) are known worldwide for their contributions to innovation and research.

India's culture is a big part of its identity. It is the origin of Hinduism, Buddhism, Jainism, and Sikhism. It is a very spiritual place, but also embraces different religions, languages, and traditions. With 22 official languages and over 1,600 dialects, India's languages are some of the most varied in the world. Bollywood makes more movies than

Hollywood. Indian books, music, art, and food continue to influence the world, making India a major cultural force.

Women have played a key role in India's political and social changes. Indira Gandhi became the country's first female prime minister in 1966, leading the way for other women. Women are having more say in India's economy, politics, and society, though there are still problems with gender equality and getting women into the workforce. The country has made progress in supporting women's rights, with policies that help education, business, and women's participation in government.

As the world's biggest democracy, India has over 900 million voters. Even though its political system can be complicated, it has always supported democratic values, a free press, and independent courts. Despite its size and variety, India has been a stable democracy since 1947, thanks to its strong institutions and active citizens.

India's growing importance has led to increased collaboration with the Nordic countries. They share interests in technology, sustainability, and innovation, which has strengthened relationships. From joint projects in green energy and smart cities to research and cultural exchanges, they work together in the pursuit of solutions to global problems.

India is an ever-evolving nation with deep roots in culture and diversity. Its ability to balances economic growth with social progress, sustainability, and working with the world will shape the future of India and the world.

Chapter 2
The Gender Bridge

India and the Nordic countries share a robust and growing partnership, grounded in their mutual commitment to sustainability, technological innovation, and inclusive economic development. Over the last 10 years, India and the Nordic countries have worked closely, leading to more trade, investments, and research partnerships. They collectively focus on green energy, reusing materials, and using digital tech, which makes this partnership important for global progress.

The first Nordic-India Summit in Stockholm in 2018 brought together Prime Minister Narendra Modi and the prime ministers of Sweden, Norway, Denmark, Finland, and Iceland to boost trade, innovation, and sustainability efforts. The summit was centred on working together on clean energy, digitalization, and ocean cooperation, which was a big step in strengthening India-Nordic ties.

The Second India-Nordic Summit happened in May 2022 in Copenhagen, Denmark. Prime Minister Narendra Modi met with the Prime Ministers of Denmark, Iceland, Finland, Sweden, and Norway. The summit focused on working together on world peace and security, climate change, renewable energy, innovation, and digitalization. The leaders discussed the situation in Ukraine, with emphasis on the need to respect international law. They also agreed to work more on environmental sustainability, the ocean economy, and international groups, with the Nordic countries promising to support India becoming a permanent member of a changed UN Security Council.

In March 2024, India and the European Free Trade Association (EFTA)—which includes Switzerland, Norway, Iceland, and Liechtenstein—signed a significant Trade and Economic Partnership Agreement (TEPA). This agreement is supposed to remove most of the taxes on industrial products to facilitate trade. The EFTA countries have committed to invest $100 billion more in India over the next 15 years, which sought to create a million jobs there. The TEPA also talks about sustainable growth and protecting ideas, which is important for India's trade with European countries.

Since 2023, the Indian Danish Chamber of Commerce and Industry, the Sweden-India Business Council, Finland Chamber of Commerce in India, Invest India, and Det Moderne India have worked together on Indo-Nordic summits and roundtables. These events have been conducted online and in person, including in Delhi and at the World Economic Forum in Davos. Other NGOs have also been invited to participate, making the discussion more collaborative.

The Third India-Nordic Summit is expected to be in Oslo, Norway, in 2025. Building on what they have already done in the past, this meeting is to continue to improve the partnership between India and the Nordic countries. The focus is expected to be on renewable energy, innovation, climate change, and sustainable growth. Leaders will also talk about world issues, like peace and security, and explore ways for deeper economic ties and growth for both sides.

Gender Equality and Social Impact

Both India and the Nordic nations believe gender equality is a key to economic and social progress. The Nordics are leaders in making workplaces fair for women, having good parental leave policies, and paying people equally, which is a good example of India's changing job market.

India has made progress in female entrepreneurship, increased number of girls and women studying science and math, and being in politics, but still needs to close gender gaps in the workforce. The Nordic countries and India are working together to encourage women in leadership, give them more access to money, and train them in rural and urban areas.

Tradition and Change: Women in the Nordics

The Nordic region's gender equality is the result of years of hard work. Historically, like much of the world, Nordic societies were very patriarchal, with strict gender roles that did not give women many chances in public or private. Men controlled land and government, while women were expected to focus on the home, children, and helping with family businesses.

The 20th century brought big changes because of economic needs, political movements, and society becoming more modern. The Nordic welfare system, which started in the mid-20th century, put gender equality at its core, making women's rights important for the nation's economic success. New policies changed women's roles, letting them work, go to school, and make their own choices like never before.

Important Moments for Women's Rights in the Nordics

Here are some key moments that shaped the Nordic approach to gender equality:

Access to Birth Control: The birth control pill in the 1960s gave women control over their bodies, allowing them to plan their careers, have kids later, and make their own life choices without worrying about unplanned pregnancies.

Easier Divorce: In the early 20th century, it was hard to get divorced in the Nordics, and the laws usually favoured men. But in the 1970s, laws changed to make divorce easier, so women had the legal and financial help to leave bad marriages without being left with nothing. This was a big step for women which helped them become independent, especially in cases of abuse or financial control.

Free Education: One of the most important things about the Nordic system is that education is free for everyone. By making sure girls had the same opportunities as boys, the region created a skilled female workforce that helped the economy grow and innovation thrive. In the Nordics, in contrast to men, more women attend higher education, although men continue to dominate STEM fields, with women making up only about one-third of STEM graduates.

More Women in the Workforce: The female labour force participation in Nordic countries (like Sweden and Norway) is around 70%, among the highest globally. Women in Sweden, Norway, Denmark, Finland, and Iceland have access to good childcare, parental leave, and flexible work, so it's easier to balance work and family life.

Good Parental Leave Policies: The Nordic model is known for its parental leave system. Unlike other places where maternity leave is short or unpaid, the Nordic countries are renowned for their generous parental leave policies, promoting gender equality and active participation of both parents in child-rearing. This makes sure women do not have to do all the childcare, so they can go back to work sooner and not have to stop their careers. Giving fathers a part of the parental leave has helped change attitudes, making it normal for men to be caregivers and promoting gender equality at home and at work.

Breaking Barriers in Politics

The Nordics have also led the way in women's participation in politics. In the region, women got the right to vote earlier than in many other parts of the world:

- Finland (1906): The first country to give women the right to vote and run for parliament.

- Norway (1913): One of the first to let women vote.

- Denmark and Iceland (1915): They followed soon after.

- Sweden (1921): Women got full voting rights.

One of the most important moments in Iceland was electing Vigdís Finnbogadóttir in 1980. She was the world's first democratically elected female president, which changed how people thought about women in leadership.

During her 16 years as president, she was a strong advocate for women's education, cultural diplomacy, and protecting the environment. She inspired many Icelandic women to get into politics, business, and education, showing that women could be good leaders.

Her election came after the Women's Strike of 1975 when 90% of Icelandic women didn't work, cook, or take care of their children for a day to show how important they were. The strike brought the country to a stop and made the government take action on gender equality. It led to key laws being changed, including forming the Women's Alliance, a political party focused on women's rights.

Gro Harlem Brundtland became Norway's first female Prime Minister in 1981, paving the way for many others. More recently, Sanna Marin of Finland and Katrín Jakobsdóttir of Iceland have shown that modern female leadership in the Nordic region is non-discriminatory and respects gender equality.

The Economic and Social Outcome

The Nordic countries have seen high employment, good social security, and economic growth because they have allowed women to fully participate in the workforce.

Studies indicate that enhancing women's participation in the workforce leads to higher GDP growth, poverty reduction, and increased innovation. For instance, closing gender employment gaps could boost global GDP by 20%. Additionally, achieving gender parity in the workforce could add up to $28 trillion to annual global GDP by 2025.

Gender equality has also led to higher birth rates compared to other developed regions. While countries like Japan and Italy struggle with aging populations because of low birth rates, the Nordics have kept their birth rates fairly stable. This is because women do not have to choose between career and family—which is facilitated by progressive and equitable social policies.

Challenges and the Future

Despite the progress, gender equality in the Nordics still has a way to go. Women are still underrepresented in top jobs, and biases still affect hiring and promotions. The Nordic Paradox—the idea that even in gender-equal societies, gender gaps still exist in certain fields—is a topic for debate.

With globalization, migration, and changing workplaces, new challenges are emerging. Promoting diversity beyond gender—including ethnicity, and social background—will be an important topic in the current discussions on Nordic equality.

A Model for the World

The Nordic countries have shown that gender equality has positive effects for the economy and society. Policies that support women help everyone, not just individuals, but also businesses, families, and nations.

As other countries try to copy the Nordic model, here's a key insight: change takes time. It requires legal reforms, economic policies, and cultural shifts. The Nordics didn't get gender equality by accident—it was the result of years of activism, political will, and believing that equal societies are stronger.

The journey from patriarchy is still ongoing, but the Nordics have given a blueprint to the rest of the world. If other nations are willing to invest in gender equality, they can build fairer and more prosperous societies.

From Patriarchy to Progress: The Evolving Role of Women in India

For centuries, India has been a male-dominated society with unfair treatment of women in and outside of families. Women are traditionally expected to get married. The dowry tradition makes people see daughters as a financial burden. In India, many births are at home, so they are not always registered.

The Indian government has tried to enact laws against treating women unfairly with limited results due to social and economic differences especially in rural areas. However, conditions improved in the last decade due to legislative changes. The 2005 Hindu law gave daughters the same inheritance rights as sons. The growing trend is that more women keep their maiden names after marriage. This way, they do not lose their identity nor forfeit inheritance and marital rights. Families without sons are also becoming less dependent on their sons-in-law for financial stability, leading to greater acceptance of divorce, particularly in major cities.

The opportunities for women have grown, especially for those who belong to the middle class. However, for poor women, finding these opportunities remains challenging.

India has the lowest female workforce participation rate in the world. An increase in women's workforce participation and income could lead to faster economic growth, reduced poverty, and greater prosperity. Not only will the women benefit from this, but their husbands and children will as well.

Strong Women in Bollywood

In traditional Indian cinema, women were seen as pure and family-like. This idea of women is changing. In the past decade, Indian cinema has produced a series of films that challenge this view of woman in society. These modern films tell audiences of the stories and struggles of women.

Films like *English Vinglish* and *Queen* have changed the narrative that women are always co-dependent. The movies' characters show the lives of women through the lens of tradition versus modern ideals.

One especially important film was 2013's *Queen* starring Kangana Ranaut. This film shows a young woman who, after being jilted by her husband-to-be, becomes independent and travels the world. As she travels to Paris and beyond, she learns about herself. The film teaches women about the agency to save themselves and to move forward.

Recent films overall, now unveil the struggles women face because of sociocultural concepts such as tradition, culture and love. Viewers now want to see women who are realistic, strong and relatable on screen.

Movies like Mrs., *Piku*, *Queen* and *English Vinglish* which place women at the center of their narrative have been widely successful. This proves that if the story is good and realistic, then it works with Indian audiences.

This trend indicates a shift in the general perception of women. Bollywood now portrays Indian women who are strong, confident, independent and who take charge of their lives. They no longer need to be saved.

Bridging the Gender Divide

India has for years been a primarily patrilineal society. This reality can also be seen in Indian business and corporate culture, from small enterprises to large corporations.

Multiple generations of families live together, and are all involved in the family business. Sons are usually given business responsibilities and told the path to follow to become successful.

There are social class structures in India. This caste system is not easily changed.

Being a *First and Only* person, company or NGO means leading change for the betterment of society. Most people like to stick with what they know and what they like, but there are others who understand that old methods do not work anymore.

These pioneers influence attitudes and enlighten others about the advantages of progress. By increasing awareness, the traditional opinion will change.

If there is enough support for the idea, these pioneers can transform mindsets. As a result, the society experiences changes that make it fairer and more equal.

Many countries have benefited from women's rights. It is important to the whole society because when women are free to exercise more rights, the society is better for it. It takes time to teach everyone the importance of understanding and supporting women's rights. Societies need to work with each other.

The coming chapters will highlight the need to bridge the gender divide between the Nordics and India.

There is more to the divide between India and the Nordic nations than equality. It also has an impact on innovation, inclusivity, and economic prosperity.

Nordic countries understand equality. They create laws that support everyone. India continues to face significant challenges in achieving gender equality, with women encountering obstacles in leadership, employment, and education. For instance, only 8% of CEOs in Indian organizations are women, highlighting a substantial gender disparity in leadership roles. In terms of employment, women's participation in the formal workforce remains low, with only about a quarter of women engaged in formal employment. Educational disparities are also evident; approximately 62% of women have received no schooling at all, compared to 31% of men, contributing to ongoing challenges in achieving gender parity.

India and the Nordic nations are very different when it comes to gender equality. Both, nonetheless, have important things to teach us. The Nordics can understand India's approach to progress in a diverse and complex society, and India can learn from Nordic policies. A more successful and equitable future for both areas can be achieved if they work together.

Women in Leadership

Despite their vastly different histories, India and the Nordic nations have one thing in common: very few women are able to rise to positions of high leadership. Few women reach senior positions or the top of the corporate ladder, despite the fact that many begin their careers at the entry level.

Research shows that eliminating the disparity will improve overall business profitability in addition to giving women equal opportunities. Firms work more effectively when men and women collaborate in leading, research suggests. Diversified leadership teams make firms innovate, spurs superior decision-making, and creates a more congenial and productive workplace environment.

Through investment in education that balances academic knowledge and hands-on skill-building, India and the Nordics can turn gender equality into a transformative reality. However, achieving this requires addressing one of the biggest barriers to progress—the difficulty of hiring and retaining women in the workforce.

The next section of this book delves into the challenges Indian women face in the workplace, from cultural and societal barriers to structural biases within companies. Through insights from experts and business leaders we explore practical solutions for employers to attract and retain female talent. This book brings together key stakeholders to raise global awareness about gender diversity and encourages both regions to reflect on their own systems and best practices. By working together, India and the Nordics can build a more inclusive and gender-equal future, one where economic growth and innovation benefit from the full participation of women.

Chapter 3

Seema Arora on Policy and Societal Change

Seema Arora advocates for equality between genders and is working towards enabling an ecosystem that can increase women's involvement in decision-making process and in workplaces. She believes that women need to have a complete understanding of their goals and that they need to take steps to overcome obstacles to unlock new opportunities. Her observations on India's progress underpin the significance of policies, social attitudes, and corporate culture in influencing women's greater participation in economic activities.

Seema perceives the working women gap in India as a paradox. Although 53% of women are employable, just 32% are employed in comparison to 76% of men. This disparity indicates profound challenges. Yet, one has seen improvement by all three drivers - government, private sector, and society - though still uneven and needing steady attention.

Enabling Government Policies and Laws

Government policies have contributed to minimizing workplace gender disparities, Seema shares. Through the Maternity Benefit Amendment Act of 2017, the government increased paid maternity leave duration from 12 weeks to 26 weeks which benefited women by simplifying their work-life balance. Employed workers can access child facilities at the workplace and this has led to an increase in working mothers as they can now combine employment with appropriate childcare.

Numerous laws have been passed by the Indian Parliament to protect women at work. Under the Sexual Harassment of Women at Workplace (Prevention, Prohibition and Redressal) Act, also known as the POSH Act, women can work in an environment where harassment is prohibited so they can perform their jobs without hesitation. According to the Equal Remuneration Act, women should receive equal pay for equal work, thereby upholding workers' appreciation value during pay determination, irrespective of the gender. The participation of women in organizational boards together with Panchayati Raj institutions creates leadership opportunities that were previously unavailable. Village panchayats provide reserved seats to women, so they can be empowered to attend to problems and shape governance. Grassroots-level women leaders are bringing about change, rewriting patriarchal perceptions, and influencing their societies.

Industry's Critical Role in Enhancing Opportunities

Though effective, these efforts are only the beginning, Seema points out. The private sector needs to close the gap between practice and law. A survey revealed that fewer than 5% of India's Fortune 100 companies had women in senior positions, while more than half of women wanted to be leaders, pointing to the need for more robust measures.

One reason behind this could be that firms tend to stereotype roles and believe that women value caregiving over careers. This restricts development and perpetuates gender lines. Seema Arora suggests that to promote inclusiveness, organizations need to break these conventions and actively engage women in defining their career trajectories, providing equal growth opportunities. Mentorship and sponsorship initiatives assist women in breaking down barriers and self-doubt. Mentors steer them through difficult situations, whereas sponsors facilitate career advancement. "Shadow roles" enable women to temporarily take the lead, improving confidence and combating imposter syndrome. She highlights that these initiatives prepare women for leadership, resulting in more representation and inclusivity in the workplace.

India's corporate landscape has evolved, with Fast-Moving Consumer Goods companies recognizing workplace gender diversity. As women form a large customer base, firms now prioritize hiring them in marketing, product design, and staff roles to better serve this large customer base. This shift also reflects a broader trend of leveraging diverse perspectives for a competitive advantage.

Supporting Women Leaders in Rural India

Challenges still abound in expanding women's involvement in small and medium-sized enterprises because of scarce resources and consciousness. The urban-rural gap also adds to gender inequality, Seema notes. Nevertheless, despite these challenges, some of India's most motivational women leaders have emerged from rural India.

Women leaders emerging from the development sector in rural India constantly battle against challenges in initiating community-level socio-economic change. The Confederation of Indian Industry's (CII) 'Women Exemplar Program' identifies these change leaders from far-flung locations and facilitates them in driving meaningful actions in the areas of education, health, and livelihood.

Held back by cultural practices in rural communities, women have struggled to bring education within reach, particularly for girls. CII, through the Women Exemplar Program, helps women leaders establish and manage local schools, ending the cycle of poverty in several regions. Similarly, women's healthcare projects, launched through the CII initiative in multiple locations, have contributed towards enhanced maternal and child health indicators. Most women leaders in India are not politicians but admired members of society known for their commitment. Collectively, they are a large pool of change agents, touching the lives of millions and advancing social change through their initiatives. Their efforts show the strength of women in bringing about positive change.

Leveraging the Demographic Opportunity

India's 440+ million millennials hold immense untapped potential with a focus on workplace gender diversity. Young women increasingly desire high-calibre careers and leadership positions.

Companies need to change policies and launch programs that enable women's aspirations and at the same time, ensures a diverse and high-performing workforce.

A diverse workplace flourishes with flexibility, support and inter-respect. Offering flexible working hours enables women to strike a balance between work and personal life, while sound support systems such as maternity leave and childcare services enable working mothers to stay on the job. In addition to policies, making a culture of respectful work reinforces the point that every worker matters. Regulatory authorities possess vital responsibilities to eliminate system-based biases together with subconscious biases for building equitable environments. Value for diversity creates situations where organizations achieve maximum productivity and innovation while getting the best performance from their people.

The progress of gender diversity throughout India demonstrates growing respect for women, along with societal changes. The remaining distance between aspiration and chance is however, still significant. According to Seema, to achieve real gender diversity, the government, corporate sector, and society need to make consistent efforts to substitute traditional norms with progressive thoughts.

Increasing synergy between the government, industry captains, and social policy think tanks offers immense promise and the combined force can intensify individual and collective action to deliver change from below. Public-private partnerships for skills development can make women fit for work, whereas corporate-NGO collaborations can create a mosaic of diversity and inclusion that can set new standards for advances.

India is at a juncture where its pool of talent, young human capital, and increasing consciousness about gender diversity can help women realize their potential. Economic development, social advancement, and cultural change are within reach by making space for women to contribute without obstruction. Gender equity is not about numbers and legislation—it is about building a world where all have the opportunity to flourish. Seema Arora states that women need to be empowered to contribute at every level, from executive boardrooms to panchayats in villages, with their contribution acknowledged in crafting a sustainable tomorrow.

Making Diversity an Intrinsic Part of Business Strategy

Through its Centre for Women Leadership, CII leads the advancement of women in the workplace by delivering training programs to female executives while facilitating gender-sensitive enterprise ventures implementing sex equality assessment procedures and facilitating gender cognition development. These strategic initiatives make efforts to help both infrastructural and cultural barriers so work environments can introduce lasting gender equality.

Indian women remain distant from achieving gender equality based on current data: A little more than 18% senior leadership roles filled by women in 2024 and with only 26.8% representation in the overall workforce in 2024. These figures indicate both obstacles and room for improvement.[57] The perception of diversity as an HR requirement and not a business asset is a critical issue. Seema Arora emphasizes that genuine advancement occurs when diversity becomes an intrinsic part of business strategy.

True gender diversity means more than just numbers—men have to acknowledge the value that women bring to the workplace. Correlating diversity with quantifiable parameters creates a culture of inclusion and celebration. One of the biggest challenges is the double burden of women—developing professionally while carrying family responsibilities. Most women leave or disconnect from decision-making and active workplace involvement due to these demands.

Policies such as longer maternity leave and on-site crèche can help address this issue. Another obstacle is the fundamentally ingrained societal attitudes. In order to truly attain gender equality, change in workplace policies is not enough; a deeper cultural transformation is required in terms of societal prejudices, family attitudes and household responsibilities.

Drivers of Change

Such advances are primarily being fuelled by increased participation of women in the service economy, such as finance, retail, and online commerce. All these sectors are now major agents of gender diversity, providing women not just jobs, but also means to reach leadership positions and career advancement.

Another major factor driving women's advancement in India is the increased focus on STEM—science, technology, engineering, and mathematics. Coupled with fast-paced digitization, this is a perfect setup for high-achieving professionals. The COVID-19 pandemic sped up digital embracement across sectors, opening up new avenues for women in fintech, EdTech, AI, and other new-age sectors.

The transition from internal combustion engines to electric vehicles in the transportation and automotive sectors opens new doors for women. With mechanical systems being replaced by electronic systems, the field has become gender neutral. Seema Arora sees this change as a key contributor. A strategic move at this stage can dramatically increase opportunities for women, she points out.

India's advancement in bringing women into top leadership has been fuelled by planned campaigns and efforts at gender-neutral work environments, mentorship, and leadership development. These initiatives have been a huge help in career advancement for women and in assuming leadership positions. Firms now deploy shadow roles for women, where they occupy leadership positions on an interim basis and perform critical tasks. This increases confidence levels, overcomes imposter syndrome, and develops the talent pool.

Seema Arora believes India can learn valuable lessons from the Nordic nations due to their well-known achievements in gender equality. In her view, cross-cultural exchange provides the ability to drive positive transformation. The CII facilitates knowledge exchange between India and the Nordic nations through joint projects as well as mutual engagement with similar challenges and optimization of best practices.

Policy innovation together with work-life balance and parental leave functions as the strategic areas that have successfully cultivated gender equality across the Nordic nations. Transforming these inclusive approaches to match Indian social economic fabric and cultural values will facilitate the path towards gender equality.

According to Seema Arora, India's rapid digitization in payments and commerce, has shown to the world the country's digital ecosystem prowess and at the same time, provided a valuable blueprint for other countries to replicate. She further highlights technology's potential to drive meaningful change and believes that it has the ability to create a worldwide ecosystem based on learning, cooperation and best practices – uniting countries in their pursuit for gender equality.

Collaboration is Key

Seema's career path is an example of the role organizational support plays in empowering women. Having spent more than 30 years at CII, she remembers how flexible work arrangements allowed her to balance work and family. This forward-thinking precedent provides insight into contemporary workplaces. Now, as a leader, she is actively mentoring and promoting workplace policies that benefit the next generation so that women can be given the opportunities and flexibility they need to succeed.

India's journey towards gender equity is marked both by challenges and opportunities. The recent demographic turnaround, with more girls than boys, bodes well for the country's future. Further, the rising number of women at senior management levels demonstrates that breakthroughs are possible with policy alignment, organizations' determination, and an evolving society.

Nonetheless, attaining genuine gender balance in C-suite positions requires ongoing effort, active measures, and readiness to confront the status quo. Organizations have to institute mentorship initiatives, leadership development, and develop policies that allow women to rise through the corporate ranks. India can be a world leader in gender diversity and inclusion. To achieve this, it needs to leverage its huge workforce, foster innovative solutions, and enhance global partnerships that propel sustainable change.

Seema Arora rightly observes, "Every individual has a role to play. If we treat everybody as equal and offer opportunities to everybody, it is possible to create a society in which gender equality is a normal way of life. Then there shouldn't be any need for any discussions on the topic." She points out that gender equality can be achieved through collective effort from individuals, organizations, and society. She also points out the necessity of going beyond discussion and embracing tangible action that ensures inclusiveness. By being fair to everyone and doing away with biases, societies can establish a culture where gender equality is not something to be wished for but a natural phenomenon.

Chapter 4

Ritu Kumar on HR Practices and Company-Level Challenges

At COWI India, Ritu Kumar, who spearheads the People & Organisation for India, Lithuania, and Poland and the Global People's Services unit, has been committed to building an open and pro-women work environment. She has been instrumental in implementing varied employee-driven initiatives in the direction of improving workplace policy and building a more nurturing working environment. She is a visible leader with a firm commitment to driving diverse talent both into and within the industry.

Challenges in hiring women

Ritu Kumar's efforts have played a pivotal role in confronting the specific challenges that come with hiring women in India. She understands these challenges go beyond the recruitment process and run deeply on the levels of cultural, social, and institutional barriers. Most women have a hard time balancing career goals with what society expects from them, whereas companies grapple with gender biases, even unconscious ones, influencing hiring.

With her long-standing experience in organizational development and HR, Ritu offers constructive advice on overcoming these impediments. She calls for formal mentorship programs, adaptable work plans, and leadership roles that give women self-confidence at every career stage. Her contributions form part of the greater scheme of promoting workplaces that not only welcome gender diversity but nurture it as well. By addressing recruitment issues in their entirety, she is contributing to the formation of a more inclusive and progressive Indian corporate world.

These barriers most typically arise in the early life of a female scholar, being a product of cultural expectations as well as socially embedded gender paradigms. The majority of women are driven to pursue work related to acceptability in a social context rather than self-interest.

Civil engineering presents an interesting illustration of this kind of under-representation, a profession that is historically perceived and projected to be for men because of sex-related stereotypes, in addition to gender-insensitive environments. Female engineers are frequently disadvantaged in working conditions with insufficient facilities to suit their needs, discouraging talented women from seeking employment in these areas. The lack of such supportive policies and facilities discourages capable women from pursuing careers in engineering, perpetuating inequalities. Responding to such limitations with conducive policies and company improvements is important for providing equal opportunities for women in engineering and more.

Even with firms such as COWI embracing merit-based, progressive recruitment practices, the small number of female candidates complicates the recruitment process. Ritu Kumar emphasizes the necessity of a proactive strategy, working in partnership with educational institutions to spot and encourage high-potential female students to join the industry.

Even with India's huge student population, the number of women entering traditionally male-dominated professions is disproportionately low. Recruitment, however, is only the first obstacle. As women move through various stages of life, new issues emerge, tending to limit their career advancement. Societal pressures, family care responsibilities, and workplace prejudices also impede their professional advancement. Overcoming these obstacles needs concerted efforts in mentoring, policy changes, and work flexibility to allow women to excel at every level of their career.

At the entry level, about 20-22% of civil engineering personnel are female candidates. The proportion declines precipitously at middle management levels, where career advancement is frequently associated with marriage and childbearing. These transitions take a major toll on women's career development, resulting in the widely documented "broken pipeline" effect.

Ways to overcome challenges

Unless they are supported by workplace policies and cultural change, most women are forced out of the labour force or cannot climb the career ladder. Consequently, leadership positions are still largely occupied by men, reinforcing gender disparities and restricting diversity at the decision-making level. To overcome this, there is a need for interventions that are focused, like mentorship schemes, flexible work patterns, and inclusive leadership development to enable women to keep climbing the career ladder without giving up personal commitments.

It is said by Ritu that ensuring that there are more females in civil engineering and keeping them with the company during their careers is still a huge challenge. Organizations need to address the entire career path of a woman—from learning and initial career growth, mid-career vtransition, to leadership positions—with a holistic strategy.

This calls for proactive steps in the form of mentorship schemes, flexible workplaces, gender-sensitive facilities, and work-life balance support policies. By creating an inclusive environment and equal growth opportunities, organizations can see to it that women enter and succeed and climb up the career ladder in the field of civil engineering.

This entails enacting policies that offer women the support and sympathy they need at such milestone stages of life while actively promoting gender equity. Such milestones as marriage, motherhood, and caregiving have a defining impact on the life course of a woman. Aware of this, organizations such as COWI not only pay attention to hiring female candidates but also to retaining them by tackling the issues that arise at these essential stages.

One of the main strategies at COWI is to create awareness and empathy among managers. Line managers are trained to have open, supportive discussions with women employees at critical points in time like pregnancy and childcare. This helps in creating a more inclusive and empathetic workplace, enabling women to progress in their careers with confidence and support.

Policies at COWI

Managers usually are in doubt regarding;

"When should you inquire about a female colleague's maternity leave arrangements?"

"How do I talk about the handover procedure?"

COWI helps managers improve their skills in respectful communication through the guidance they receive from the organization. The "return-to-work" program at COWI begins during pregnancy as one of its critical initiatives. The program gives maternal support through educational content to female employees. The organization suggests that managers maintain an open dialogue with employees on maternity leave to prevent detachment from their groups and organizational activities. This practice builds inclusiveness while reducing workplace isolation to ensure successful work re-entry for women after maternity leave.

COWI bases its return-to-work support for women upon high organizational flexibility. The workplace transition presents mothers with two types of challenges because they need to handle childcare issues together with addressing feelings of guilt and their doubts about their professional abilities. The company provides work-from-home flexibility and adaptable work hours, which allow female employees to gradually rejoin their careers.

Ritu remembers one outstanding case where a colleague was promoted while on maternity leave. Taken aback by the chance, the colleague asked if her leave would affect her chance to assume the new position. Ritu assured her that maternity leave and performance have nothing to do with each other—potential and ability determine suitability for a position. This is one-way COWI demonstrates that it sees women's life cycles as part of their career path and not an obstruction to career advancement.

Creating an inclusive workplace is not just about policies—it is about a culture change. In COWI, raising awareness among male colleagues is the first step in creating a friendly work environment. Men are urged to take an active role in sharing domestic duties, allowing women to concentrate on their careers without being overwhelmed. This culture change is important in creating a balanced and equal workplace.

COWI has also implemented Nordic-style practices, such as relying on trust rather than strict legal entitlements in granting sick leave. In India, where leave policies tend to be strictly enforced, this flexible mindset is focused on employee health. The company also provides paternity leave to motivate men to become more actively involved in childcare. These practices have a dual benefit—less burden on women for round-the-clock childcare and shared family responsibility.

Another decisive factor that strengthens women to move into careers is exposure to workplace settings and accessibility to ongoing training. In COWI, women workers have the opportunity to work on worldwide projects, with which they experience valuable exposure to various work conditions. The corporation also provides upskilling modules for individuals aspiring to increase their knowledge and skills. These programs not only encourage professional development but also enable women to gain confidence and widen their professional spheres.

For women returning to work after maternity leave, COWI provides a well-structured reboarding program designed to ease their transition. This includes specialized courses that enhance both technical proficiency and soft skills like communication. Additionally, they are given opportunities to apply their expertise to complex global projects. Through this initiative, COWI ensures that women feel supported and confident in resuming their careers, enabling them to reintegrate seamlessly despite their time away. Global projects present turning-point experiences, especially for women employed in Denmark or Norway. Such experience fuels motivation, enhances self-worth, and strengthens professional abilities while expanding their outlook. Thus, they obtain increased clarity of purpose in laying out their careers for the longer term.

Ritu emphasizes that such exposure provides valuable learning moments, enabling women to gain confidence and hone expertise in niche disciplines, ultimately gaining strength to improve their careers with renewed purpose.

Getting a job is only the initial challenge; the actual task is retention and career growth, which can prove to be the most challenging part of the experience. Most women are subjected to workplace prejudices and veiled taunts that render the work environment toxic. In India, almost half of employed women are subject to such prejudices, further adding to their stress. Already burdened with domestic duties, such workplace issues dissuade them further from advancing their professional lives, making career growth even more challenging.

Ritu acknowledges that although she has been privileged to work in positive settings, there are still many women who face significant obstacles. Gender, age, and looks tend to heighten workplace prejudices, making women work twice as hard to demonstrate their abilities. At the same time, domestic duties remain relatively static, making it challenging for women to concentrate on their careers. This double burden adds a further layer of hardship, constraining their chances of professional development and career progression.

For sustainable gender diversity, organizations need a whole-system approach. Ritu identifies three key pillars:

1. ***Ecosystem*** – This includes infrastructure and policies that enable women, like flexible work and parental leave.

2. ***Environment*** – This includes values and culture within the organization, with a very strong focus on respect and inclusion.

3. ***Engagement*** – This is about giving work, development opportunities, and ongoing learning.

The woman leader must be more than a "diversity candidate." Instead, their emergence must be identified and celebrated based on the exclusive values and perceptions they bring to the table. Gender diversity becomes a reality where biases are resolved while creating performance-oriented cultures in which talent and contribution are distinguished from stereotypes.

Ritu looks back at her experience, stressing the need to seek assistance and establish networks. She urges women to seek assistance and form support groups in their workplaces. As a leader, she attempts to pay back the support she has received by mentoring and empowering other female workers.

The recruitment and retention of women in India are complex challenges that need to be addressed at both the individual and institutional levels. Organizations such as COWI show that with firm determination, committed action, inclusive policies, and cultural change, workplaces can become more supportive of women's success.

Organizations can realize their workforce's full potential by:

1. Overcoming systemic barriers

2. Building a supportive and inclusive culture

3. Investing in women's professional growth and development

The formation of support networks at work becomes essential, according to Ritu, since it helps women obtain assistance while building organizational communities. She dedicates herself to executive roles in which she provides mentoring to women team members. Organizations in India need staff retention programs, together with personal initiatives, to increase women's participation in their workforce. COWI, together with other companies, demonstrates that effective workplace gender diversity programs result from combining inclusive policies with cultural transformations and leadership engagement. Organizations that eliminate obstacles and establish supportive environments alongside investing in female professionals enable their workforce to reach its true potential while driving permanent success.

Chapter 5
Sohini Mishra on What Women Want

Women who were born between the early 1980s and mid-1990s, also referred to as Gen Y or millennials, are standing at the forefront of change and forging a paradigm shift in India's future. They are career-oriented, socially conscious, and environmentally friendly, making a difference throughout the nation. Over the last decade, women have had increased access to higher education, done well in their respective fields and sometimes even out-performed men. This change presents a significant question: What do women desire?

To learn the dreams and woes of working urban women, we speak with Sohini Mishra, Founder of Women in the Hood, a hyper-local community for women piloting the project in Gurgaon. Sohini feels that unattached women—divorced, separated, widowed, or unmarried—possess a distinctive opportunity to exist in a world without precedents.

What Do Women Desire?

In the contemporary changing world, solidarity and community support are not only empowering individuals but are crucial for millennial women as they face personal and professional challenges.

"We Indians never thought that we would see such a transition until the COVID-19 crisis," Sohini says. "Through the lockdown, we understood the importance of extended support systems beyond the traditional family unit to negotiate contemporary life. This gave a boost to hyper-local communities all over social media. Since 2020, such an understanding has only intensified. In that context, women-only networks are being sought more often now by more and more women in urban landscapes. By promoting collaboration, mentorship, and community action, these groups assist women in overcoming challenges and moving toward a more just society."

Programs and Policies

Through networking support, platforms and programs for women, like local solidarity groups and those that reward volunteering in the community, benefits can accrue to both individuals and society as a whole. Even though government policies are aimed at enhancing political representation, economic opportunities, and legal rights, there are some problems faced while implementing them successfully throughout India. Therefore, unattached women living in cities still face quite a few challenges.

Challenges faced by women

Safety Concerns:

Public areas and transport are not safe, compelling women to be more cautious.

Housing Bias:

Single women are often not rented to by property owners because of social prejudices.

Financial Hardships:

Limited credit and financial opportunities impact their autonomy.

Women and communities need to keep collaborating to overcome these issues and make policies responsive to the needs of single women in urban India. Sohini recounts how she lived in Mumbai for seven years, sharing anecdotes that highlight the plight of single women when they try to rent a flat.

"Even in Mumbai, which is renowned for being women-friendly, being a single woman tenant is rather daunting. These housing societies have approval committees typically dominated by middle-aged gentlemen who conduct interviews to determine if a single woman can be accepted as a tenant. These happen once or twice a month, and they resemble an ordeal of endurance through a barrage of unnecessary personal inquiries. Only the 'last lady standing' scores the flat. Sadly, in 2025, this process persists," she explains.

Not so long ago, women had to provide a male guarantor or co-applicant to obtain any loan, with no regard for their age, financial well-being, or credit record. Today, although women's labour force participation in India is at a level of 30%, Gen-Y women also have to combat numerous challenges in the workplace. Sohini points out some of the issues that persist - widespread leadership bias, insufficient proper facilities at workplace, absence of opportunities for networking and lack of career progression plans.

These challenges stem from recruitment and gender biases. However, the biggest hurdle is society's expectation that women must prioritize domestic roles. Many still see women's careers as personal ambitions rather than contributions to household income, overlooking the need for equal support. To shatter these shackles, a whole-of-society approach is required. "Mentorship, flexible work arrangements, mental health care, and gender equality are essential to add more women to India's workforce," Sohini outlines. "Individual development, workplace backing, and family support are all important."

The number of unattached women in India is increasing, with numbers estimated at 72 million using 2011 census figures. The exact number of single-women households in urban India is unclear, but older statistics provide some insight. A decade-old National Family Health Survey reported that about 14.1% of urban households were headed by women, including widows, divorced or separated women, and unmarried women over 35. This shift is redefining social norms, challenging traditional gender roles, and reshaping economic and domestic expectations.

The old 2011 census estimated that just 3.7% of "normal" Indian households were single-person households, both male and female. This implies that living alone was not common 14 years ago. However, these figures could have changed over time, and fresh data are required for a better picture.

Sohini, a resident of Gurgaon, sees a different world. "At least a single woman, either solo or co-resident with others, lives in every tenth house in my neighbourhood," she says. She also states that India is slowly following global trends, where career-oriented and educated, childless and unattached women would constitute 40-45% of homes in developed nations.

Summing up, no precise worldwide estimates are available, but the number of women living single is projected to increase dramatically in 2030. Reasons such as late marriages, increased rates of divorce, increased longevity, and a better emphasis on independence and careers are fuelling the trend. India is catching this worldwide trend firmly and steadfastly. This change is reshaping social norms, and challenging traditional gender roles and economic dependencies. "Single women need access to legal protection, affordable housing, safety, security, healthcare, workplace equality, and, most importantly, community support," Sohini stresses. "Women must support each other. When more women stand together, the progress we've made will lead to lasting change for future generations." But India's social psyche has not caught up as rapidly as the aspirations of millennial women. "Gen-Y women in India are ambitious, well-educated, and more empowered. But the generations that came before us have not kept up with this change," Sohini laments. It is frustrating to watch so many women being deprived of basic rights simply because long-standing social conventions go unchallenged.

Structural discrimination, gender disparity, and cultural norms still limit opportunities for women in economic, political, social, and educational fields—even in leisure, self-care, fitness, and recreation. "Women in India still don't access these spaces at the same level as men," Sohini explains.

"To bridge this gap, India needs an overall approach—a comprehensive one that prioritizes law reform, gender equality, increased access to healthcare, and pushing back against ingrained cultural practices that have shaped generations of Indian women," Sohini says. Despite these ongoing issues, India has lately seen a notable demographic change. Years of structural reforms and state interventions have led to a milestone in history. NFHS-5 (2019-21) states that India's overall sex ratio—measuring females per 1,000 males—was 1,020, the highest in history. This development is an indication of a gradual but encouraging trend towards gender equilibrium. The rise in India's overall sex ratio is largely attributed to greater female life expectancy and better gender balance among older groups. The sex ratio at birth, however, still marginally favours males. This achievement is the result of decades of campaigns against gender imbalance and the eradication of sex-based selection. But much remains to be done.

Society needs to redefine how it regards women and girls. Success for a woman is not the sole measure of her achievement in marriage, motherhood, and domesticity. Rather, India should honour achievements such as higher education, sporting excellence, professional development, and leadership roles for women at least—if not more than weddings and childbearing. In January 2025, during a girls' trip to Jaipur with a friend and her 9-year-old daughter, we passed a row of high-end jewellery and couture boutiques. Almost instinctively, the friend remarked that we must return to shop in these stores when her daughter gets married. This friend, a single mother who has struggled against all odds to create a life for herself, inadvertently reinforced the notion that weddings are the best time for extravagant purchases and celebrations. These are deeply held beliefs in our society, and Sohini insists that reimagining this narrative must start with intentional mother-daughter dialogue.

A woman's path cannot be quantified by traditional markers alone. Real success should be on her own defined terms. Women need to build judgment-free, safe spaces for one another, irrespective of age, background, or ambitions. Governments, corporations, and women leaders must actively encourage public campaigns and community programs to redefine this mindset in the long run. Though urban India has come a long way, the rural-urban gap is huge. "I think it will take decades of effort and planned implementation to bridge this rural-urban gap," Sohini admits.

Even in cities, according to Sohini, a lot more is yet to be achieved. "There is an ongoing struggle to claim that a woman's identity isn't defined only by her familial roles but also by her very existence, which is much wider and deeper," she underlines.

The Legacy of Gen-Y Women in India

The greatest legacy Gen-Y women need to leave is the strength to defy social norms and demand genuine equality. "This battle cannot cease," Sohini declares. The next generation needs to inherit a world where gender roles, sexuality, and family arrangements are not fixed. Young people need to be able to make their own decisions in a society that does not judge or exclude them. To make a difference, educated women in power need to speak openly about significant concerns such as singlehood, gender equality, financial independence, healthcare, and identity. "Their aim should be to make a society in which women's choices and experiences are respected and valued," Sohini advises.

The journey towards gender equality in India is not a straightforward one, particularly for single women with ingrained social expectations, complex conditioning and prejudices. But Gen-Y women are emerging as changemakers in their own right, fuelled by drive, determination, and responsibility. As they forge independent lives—be it in careers, financial matters, or choices of marriage—they are also helping each other and creating cohesive communities. By standing up together, fighting for equal opportunity, and confronting stereotypes, these women are setting a precedent for an open and just society. Through their efforts, not only will they have created greater opportunities for themselves, but future generations will be motivated to live unfettered and free of gender-based judgments or restrictions.

Part 2

Chapter 6
The Legacy of Breaking Barriers

Throughout history, women who are The First and Only have faced resistance—not just from the world around them but also from the invisible burdens that come with pioneering change. The cost of breaking barriers is rarely fully discussed. While society celebrates the trailblazers, their personal sacrifices, the loneliness of leadership, and the weight of representation remain largely unseen.

This section explores the complexities of resilience—not just as an individual trait but as a force that reshapes industries, policies, and cultural narratives. True perseverance is not just about defying norms; it is about ensuring that those who follow do not have to fight the same battles alone.

The women in these chapters—whether in business, activism, science, sports, or politics—have redefined what is possible for future generations. Their journeys demonstrate that resilience is not a passive endurance of hardship but an active defiance of limitations.

From challenging systemic biases to navigating male-dominated fields, these women have turned resistance into transformation. They have leveraged their struggles to build pathways for others, proving that leadership is not just about being first—it is about making sure you are not the last.

As you read their stories, consider the emotional and social costs of trailblazing. The true measure of success is not just breaking a ceiling; it is lifting others through it. The *First and Only* are not just symbols of progress—they are architects of a better future. And for that, their legacies deserve more than recognition; they deserve to be carried forward.

Chapter 7
Grit and Perseverance

Talent is a special ability that can make anyone stand out. It could be argued that extraordinary people are really ordinary people who discovered and developed their talent and kept at it until it got them somewhere. The truth is that what makes extraordinary people stand out is not just talent but perseverance. This quality, called grit, turns ambition into success. Grit, according to author and psychologist Angela Duckworth, is a combination of tenacity and desire. Grit is a weapon for change as well as a form of protection for women working in male-dominated sectors. Grit is not just a quality; it is a tool for change.

Kalpana Chawla, who was dismissed by her own father, became the first Indian woman to fly to space. She became an aerospace engineer and later joined NASA. Kalpana came from a small town where women were not encouraged to have such dreams. Yet, she braved the storm of parental and societal limitations to achieve her big dreams. Hers is a story of resilience, inspiring future generations of women.

Amal Clooney, a human rights lawyer and activist said, "Courage is contagious". Those who rise up and advocate for change always inspire others. Future generations benefited and are still benefiting from the determination shown by Kalpana. She was not afraid to go where no other Indian woman had gone, and this inspired others to believe that indeed no hurdle is too high to overcome. Norwegian marathoner Grete

Waitz is another shining example of what is possible when a woman is courageous enough to pursue her dreams against all odds. She won the New York City Marathon nine times, at a time when long-distance running was considered a male-only sport.

Grit helps women break stereotypes. It even helps them to overcome self-doubt and cultural expectations. J. Jayalalithaa overcame gender bias in Indian politics to become a respected leader in Tamil Nadu. Although this was a space dominated by men, she made herself too relevant to be ignored and built a strong political legacy. Her story proves that perseverance can redefine leadership opportunities for women in governance.

Sanna Marin, former prime minister of Finland got involved in politics to champion the cause of gender equality and pave the way for other women. All around the world, it is true that gender inclusive systems serve the purpose of developing potential talent.

Grit is important, but to be successful, women also need a supportive environment, both culturally and psychologically. This is why organizations which prioritize diversity and inclusion are crucial to female independence and development. The Nordic countries work to achieve gender equality in sectors that are pre-dominantly male. At the same time, India supports the "Beti Bachao, Beti Padhao" initiative for girls. This literally means "Save daughters, educate daughters."

Grit fuels ambition, and an inclusive environment keeps people going, allowing women to overcome obstacles and succeed. Grit is powerful, and the lives of Kalpana Chawla, Grete Waitz, and several other tenacious women are proof of this. They demonstrate how a never-give-up spirit can transform challenges into possibilities. Grit turns passion into progress and obstacles into stepping stones that help women break down barriers. When women who have grown up in a culture that stifles self-expression, break free against all odds, from those limiting beliefs, they not only redefine themselves, they pave the way for other women to do so as well. There's something powerful about a woman who hears the criticism, experiences the discrimination and bias but forges ahead anyway to carve a path for herself where she has been told that no path exists. One such woman is Sulagna Chattopadhyay. Her relentless pursuit of environmental advocacy overcame institutional bias, forced a recalibration of the system, making space for future generations.

Dr. Sulagna Chattopadhyay: A Pioneer in Climate Advocacy

Dr. Sulagna Chattopadhyay, founder and editor of Geography and You, has shaped climate discourse in India for over two decades. With nearly 30 years of experience in climate research, disaster management, and biodiversity, she has co-authored books like Climate Change and the White World and Science and Geopolitics of the White World, published by Springer. She also founded the SaGAA think tank, dedicated to polar policy and advocacy. As a leader in a male-dominated field, her journey is one of resilience, perseverance, and breaking barriers.

Navigating a Male-Dominated Field

Climate and environmental studies often attract women due to their nurturing roles in society. Women have historically led environmental movements in India, from the Chipko Movement to Narmada Bachao Andolan. Today, initiatives like Warrior Moms continue this legacy. However, representation in academia, especially in specialized fields like Polar research, remains low.

Environmental activism sees strong female leadership, but research and policy-driven fields are still male-dominated. In India, Polar research is a niche area with a select few working in this domain—fewer still are women. Also, Polar research in India is reigned by science. Social science and geopolitics find little favour. Establishing credibility in such a space has been a constant challenge. The difficulty lies not just in gender bias but in the nature of the discipline itself. Science is seen as a national priority, making it hard for non-scientific voices to be heard in environmental discourse.

As an entrepreneur, disappointment is common. Environmental work is slow-moving, and success is rare. Economic interests often overshadow conservation efforts. For instance, despite warnings about melting ice caps, industries view this as an opportunity to extract more resources rather than an urgent call for change. Research is not always neutral; it is influenced by political and financial interests. This makes advocacy an uphill battle but also reinforces the need for persistence.

The Challenge of Recognition

Women in academia face exclusion in subtle ways. While corporate spaces may openly resist female leadership, academia relies on territorialism. A case in point may be Polar scientists publishing papers on the history and geopolitics of Polar regions, attempting to push social scientists like Dr. Chattopadhyay out of the turf.

Exclusion extends beyond research. In competitive fields, powerful individuals often take credit for innovative ideas rather than fostering collaboration. Gender bias further compounds these issues, making it harder for women to establish their expertise. Ideas shared by women are often ignored until a more influential figure repeats them. In other cases, contributions are co-opted, pushing the original thinker aside. Engaging in such battles is exhausting, and at times, the best response is to move on rather than fight for recognition. The obstacles express deep institutional problems found in male-dominated professions. The battle for perseverance requires recognition of opportunities. Women must uphold personal honour, remain benign in hostile situations, and sometimes walk away, but never detract from the goal. Real transformation demands both single-minded determination and structural changes that promote comprehensive engagement.

Women in Leadership: The Unseen Struggles

Despite a rise in female visibility, it has not translated into access to opportunities for women to take leadership positions within scientific institutions. Sulagna's experience in India has led her to work with over twenty institutions across the country yet positions at the highest level remain nearly absent of female representatives. The societal bias toward gender shows in two ways through its mislabelling of female confidence as "aggressive" when men performing the same behaviour achieve a more positive response by being seen as "confident".

Sulagna's organization is women-led, with 90% of their staff being female. She posits, "I believe women must create their own spaces instead of waiting for inclusion in male-dominated fields. The resistance I face in Polar studies is subtle but persistent. Experienced scientists uphold rigid structures, keeping "outsiders" like me confined to outreach events–facilitating networking platforms for scientists rather than academic research. While I can contribute to the academic space, I am rarely invited to collaborate on research papers."

This exclusion is not unique to India. Across the world, "old boys' clubs" control access to power. Institutions may appear open, but real decisions happen behind closed doors. Even when women apply for leadership roles, selections are often predetermined. Discussing these biases openly is crucial to challenging the structures that sustain them.

The Long Road to Change

Climate action and policy reform are long-term battles. Environmental advocacy proves tiring, and advancement occurs slowly. The environmental case of defending the Delhi Ridge demonstrates the regular neglect of ecological concerns by interest groups focused on economic gains. Political figures ignore pollution discussions because they have determined that it lacks public appeal. Each small step, no matter how minutely incremental, leads toward the growth of this larger movement, though it may span several generations.

The main obstacle exists in the way scientific understanding fails to reach common public comprehension. The general public is aware of ice cap melting, yet they do not understand its direct impact on their routine activities. Effective communication is key. The feminine ability to connect emotionally with others combined with women's storytelling talents enables them to transform difficult scientific concepts into simpler explanations. Statistical information fails to motivate people to act, whereas real-life narratives successfully inspire change. The modern generation of young people passionately discuss environmental matters, yet their activism is largely confined to social media instead of grassroots activities. Digital platforms help spread knowledge, but they also lead to fewer direct actions. The challenge is to balance both—to use technology for outreach while encouraging real-world participation.

A Personal Reflection

Sulagna recounts; "There have been many moments of self-doubt. At the start of my career, I had offers from prestigious organizations, including India Today Group. They valued me, paid me well, and even kept my position open during maternity leave. Sometimes, I wonder if staying would have led to a stable career with fewer battles. But then, I remind myself why I chose this path. The struggles I face today are not just professional; they are tied to my belief in creating lasting change. Recognition from places like Norway, where I am now seen as an expert, reinforces my conviction. That validation, along with the impact of my work, reminds me that stepping away from conventional success was necessary. The fight for climate action and gender equality is difficult, but knowing I am contributing to something bigger than myself keeps me going."

Moving Forward

Women must continue stepping into leadership roles, building independent networks, and pushing past systemic barriers. Change is slow, but persistence leads to transformation. Environmental protection and policy reform are not quick fixes—they require decades of effort. Sulagna continues, "Many a time, I have felt drained by the slow pace of change. But I remind myself that nothing happens overnight. If you lose a battle today, prepare for the war tomorrow."

Looking back 100 years, we see how difficult it was for the first female lawyer, judge, or scientist. Many women before us endured harsher conditions, and their stories inspire us today. We must do the same for future generations. Women are uniquely equipped to bridge the gap between science and society. Our ability to communicate, connect, and inspire action is crucial in the fight against climate change. Every voice matter, and every effort counts. The journey is challenging, but it is also worthwhile. By staying committed, we lay the foundation for a more sustainable, equitable world.

Chapter 8
Resilience in Defiance

Psychologists and researchers have always wondered why some people thrive under the weight of personal, social or economic difficulties and others drown. Ann S. Masten, a leading researcher, calls resilience "ordinary magic". She says it's not an exceptional trait but a process of adaptability and resourcefulness.

Michael Rutter, pioneering psychologist, studied how people facing extreme adversity can adjust and even flourish. His research shows resilience is not a fixed characteristic but a dynamic mix of genetics, environment and experience. Through a gender lens, resilience gets even more complicated. Societal expectations, structural inequalities and cultural norms shape how women display resilience. Understanding these dynamics helps create inclusive spaces where resilience is not just about survival but a path to empowerment and equity.

Women have always fought for education, basic rights and justice. In India, Savitribai Phule was the first female teacher in the country. She fought against gender discrimination so that girls could go to school. She faced public ridicule and opposition, but she persisted and turned her defiance into a vision of an educated future.

Arundhati Roy does this through her writing and activism, using storytelling to expose environmental destruction, displacement and social injustice. As a writer and public intellectual, she shows us that resistance doesn't always come in the form of loud protests. Words can challenge power structures, ideas can shift public opinion, and activism can spark important conversations.

In the Nordic region, activism happens in subtle but powerful ways. Sofia Falk, transformation strategist, works on dismantling gender biases in corporate environments. Her passion for this cause drives her work forward. She strongly believes that strategic action, like the formulation and implementation of inclusive workplace policies, is what leads to real change. Sometimes, for those who dare, defiance can be costly. Ultimately, resilience is more than an act of defiance; it is not just about breaking barriers—it is about building something greater, but even this comes at a price.

The Cost of Defiance

Rina Sunder, co-founder of Det Moderne India, was raised in a culture where expectations were clearly defined—a girl's worth was tied to family honour, and her future was predetermined. Her childhood was not filled with dreams of endless possibilities but with duties—working in her father's grocery store every day after school, suppressing the longing for a life beyond it. The weight of generational customs pressed down on her, making the idea of freedom feel distant and impossible.

At home, fear was ever-present. Her father's violent outbursts toward her mother cast a long shadow over their lives, reminding them that silence and obedience were the safest choices. The constant tension, and unpredictability of rage created an environment where survival meant constantly navigating fear. Yet deep inside, she knew that life was meant to be more than simply existing. She did not want to live like her illiterate mother— She wanted freedom.

When Rina left home to study in Trondheim, it was an act of severance. She became the first and only girl in her community to leave for university. It was the moment she chose to fight for her freedom— by choosing a life that could give her the career she wanted. The consequences were swift and brutal: isolation, shame, loneliness, and rejection from her own family. She even felt like an outsider in the immigrant society in Norway. But as Viktor Frankl wrote, "Those who have a 'why' to live for can bear almost any 'how.'"

Books became her refuge—sources of strength, clarity, and transformation during a time of immense emotional turbulence. Victor Hugo's *Les Misérables*, a novel set in 19th-century France, follows the journey of Jean Valjean, a former convict seeking redemption in a society riddled with inequality. The themes of justice, endurance, and human dignity resonated deeply with her.

Equally formative was Viktor Frankl's *Man's Search for Meaning*, his memoir as a Holocaust survivor. In it, Frankl argues that life's primary motivation is not pleasure but the pursuit of meaning—even amid suffering. This notion became a compass for Rina. It reinforced her belief that purpose can be forged even in despair. Both Hugo and Frankl affirmed what she most needed to hear at the time. that hardship could be the birthplace of transformation—and that one's past need not define one's future.

Living with male roommates—an unthinkable scandal back home—was liberating, yet it brought feelings of guilt and fear.

The stories of other Indian and Pakistani girls haunted her. Some were married off when their parents took them to India or Pakistan. Some were killed for defying expectations, victims of honour killings. Others sought refuge in Nordic foster care to escape forced marriages, while some made compromises that left them feeling trapped for life. Rina refused to surrender to that fate.

Breaking off two arranged engagements and walking away from expectations to conform to a life she did not want was a turning point. The fallout was severe—her father accused her of betrayal, relatives called her names, and whispers of shame spread through the community. Yet, it was necessary for her to reclaim her autonomy. She realized that freedom wasn't just physical—it was mental and emotional, an act of survival.

In Trondheim, she found clarity and courage. She was valued for her ideas and ambition, not judged by the standards of obedience and conformity that had defined her past. But freedom came at a high cost—loneliness, guilt, and severing familiar connections with family and the challenge of being part of an immigrant society. Soon she had to bear not only her burdens but also the weight of helping to liberate her mother who her father blamed for failing as a mother.

Survival and freedom were her only goals. When Rina won the election for presidency of The International Student Festival in Trondheim (ISFiT), it was not about victory; it was about standing against every whisper of doubt and every internalized belief that she could not pursue a career in Norway. As Viktor Frankl observed, "Success, like happiness, cannot be pursued; it must ensue as the unintended side-effect of one's dedication to a cause greater than oneself." For Rina, leadership was never the goal—only the means to get her freedom.

At 22, she became the first person of colour to lead ISFiT. One of the defining moments of her life came when she sought to bring His

Holiness, the Dalai Lama, to ISFiT. Many dismissed it as impossible. But she and a fellow student refused to give up. They waited outside his door for four weeks, determined to get an answer. When His Holiness finally agreed to meet them, his words cut through her fatigue like lightning: "This is more important." In that moment, she knew her suffering and struggle meant something. H.H. Dalai Lama's acceptance of the invitation made waves in Norway, with ISFiT garnering over 800 press mentions.

While she was leading ISFiT, she was asked to help Nasim Karim, a young Pakistani girl who had been married off—the first case of forced marriage to break into Norwegian media. Norway's Ministry of Foreign Affairs required a financial sponsor and guarantor to cover Nasim's travel expenses and facilitate her return to Norway. Rina was that someone. Nasim's father happened to be her own father's best friend. The young woman had endured severe abuse from her father-in-law and her family was pressuring her to remain in her arranged marriage. When Rina met Nasim again in 2014, after more than 30 years, Nasim remembered: "You stood up for me when the whole world turned its back on me."

Strength came in small victories—a sponsorship secured, a successful debate, the belief of mentors who saw potential in her even when she doubted herself. Having friends and mentors like Knut Godager, Linda Røssland Henriksen, Gyrd Steen, Jarand Rystad, Mayor Marvin Wiseth, Rector Karsten Jacobsen, and University Director Per Ivar Maudal, along with loyal board members at ISFiT, gave her inspiration and strength. Yet, the journey was never easy. For every step forward, there were moments of guilt and sheer exhaustion as she carried both her own aspirations and a wish for a better life for her mother.

After university, she was determined to enter the private sector. In 1987, she was one of only two recruits that year at Geelmuyden Kiese (GK), one of the top consultancies alongside McKinsey and BCG. Getting in was like threading a needle. But once inside, she discovered a world where merit mattered more than background. Years later, she and her colleagues agreed: "We thought the world outside was just like GK—full of secure, intelligent men who valued competence. We didn't realize how rare that was."

In 2023, at a party hosted by Member of Parliament Himanshu Gulati, journalist Kadafi Zaman, who is three years younger than Rina, approached her. "When we were in college, we all looked up to you. You were making history with ISFiT. What you did paved the way for all of us."

For many Nordic women, freedom is a birthright taken for granted in a society that upholds individual rights. But for many Indian girls, or girls with Indian background, like Rina, freedom is something you must fight for and defend at great personal cost.

Chapter 9

Intersectionality and Identity

I was in a high-stakes boardroom meeting when I pitched an innovative strategy—only to have it ignored. Moments later, my male colleague repeated my idea, and suddenly, it was 'brilliant.' I sat there, invisible in my own success. - Rita Hansson, Senior Executive, Swedish company.

Imagine being the only woman in a meeting, where your ideas are overlooked until a male colleague repeats them—or experiencing surprise when you clearly articulate a strategy, as if competence itself were unexpected. These are examples of microaggressions: subtle yet pervasive expressions of bias that reinforce harmful stereotypes and undermine a woman's sense of competence and belonging. While many women encounter such behaviour, women of colour and those from other marginalized groups experience it more frequently and often with greater intensity. Though microaggressions may appear trivial, they are often cumulative in effect, gradually eroding confidence, inclusion, and psychological safety in professional and social spaces.

Intersectionality goes beyond just gender or ethnicity; it also about how various layers of identity influence discrimination. A woman's experience in the workplace isn't just defined by her being a woman; it also has to do with how factors like her ethnicity, background, skin colour, age, disability, and sexual orientation intersect with gender bias.

Research from McKinsey & Company and Lean revealed that Black women are more than three times as likely as white women to face surprise at their professional skills. Similarly, Asian and Latina women are twice as likely to have such experience compared to white women.

The Burden of 'Only' and 'Double Only'

Women who are the only representatives of their gender or ethnicity in leadership positions face heightened scrutiny. Their achievements and setbacks are magnified, leading to higher stress, self-monitoring, and burnout.

For women of colour, often referred to as 'Double Onlys, these challenges become even more pronounced as they deal with both racial and gender biases at the same time. Black, Latina, and Asian women often have their abilities questioned more than those of white women. Socio-economic status, caste, and religion also play a role in whether they experience discrimination. This is where intersectionality becomes relevant.

Intersectionality in Action

For every woman, the battle for gender equality looks different. Wealthy upper-caste Indian women experience gender bias, but they also enjoy privileges that are not available to Dalit women, who face sexism and caste-based oppression. A Muslim woman wearing a hijab in the Nordics or a Black woman in the Nordics experiences Islamophobia and racial bias in ways that white women do not. Despite these obstacles, many women create communities, fight systemic barriers, and promote social change. Their experiences demonstrate the severity of these disparities as well as the fortitude required to overcome them. Let us examine three women whose intersectional experiences have redefined leadership.

Stories of Intersectionality and Resilience

Kalpana Saroj proves that caste and gender discrimination can be fought—but not without immense struggle. Born into a Dalit family in Maharashtra, she defied not only societal expectations but also an abusive marriage to rise as the CEO of Kamani Tubes. Her journey proves that resilience and opportunity can overcome structural inequalities.

Environmental justice is gender justice. Vandana Shiva, a leading eco-feminist has long argued that rural women suffer most from climate change. By promoting sustainable farming practices, she connects environmental sustainability with gender equality, and ensures that marginalized women have a voice. The fact is that gender justice and social justice are linked. To fight discrimination in the workplace, we must acknowledge how sociocultural factors intersect to shape women's lives.

The Weight of Being a "Twofer": Women of Colour in Leadership

Deepa Purushothaman, a former Deloitte executive, co-founded nFormation to support diverse female leaders and challenge workplace biases. She describes the "twofer" burden—being both a woman and a person of colour—which often leads to microaggressions and exclusion.

Many women of colour report being dismissed despite success. A male colleague once told Purushothaman that she was promoted only because of diversity quotas. Others describe code switching—altering speech, dress, and behaviour to conform—only to feel further alienated. But the burden is not just professional—it's deeply personal. Women of colour don't just experience bias at work; they carry its weight home. Research links chronic exposure to workplace discrimination with long-term health effects, including anxiety, hypertension, and burnout. The stress of constantly proving oneself in an environment that questions one's legitimacy takes a silent but real toll.

Reimagining Leadership & Driving Change

Purushothaman critiques performative diversity efforts, arguing that most HR systems fail to handle racism or discrimination effectively. Real change requires structural transformation, not symbolic gestures. In her book, 'The First, The Few, The Only', she introduces "The New Rules of Power," advocating for leadership that amplifies marginalized voices instead of reinforcing outdated norms.

Workplaces will be inclusive if they:

- Create psychologically safe environments where authenticity is valued.

- Distribute leadership opportunities equitably rather than limiting women of colour to DEI-related roles.

- Hold leadership accountable for systemic bias, rather than placing the burden on marginalized individuals to "fix" workplace culture.

The real measure of inclusion is not how many diverse faces appear on a company website, but whether those voices hold power. Intersectional solutions are not an HR problem; they're a business necessity. By intentionally addressing bias, distributing leadership opportunities equitably, and making leadership accountable for institutional change, organizations can create cultures where all women—not just privileged minorities—can truly thrive.

These women's tenacity is astounding despite these exacerbated difficulties. They persevere, fight back, and create places where none previously existed. Their experiences of actively opposing and changing the systems that aim to imprison them go beyond simply enduring oppression. They demand justice, speak up, and create communities—not only for themselves but also for others who follow them. These intersecting identities must be acknowledged in the struggle for gender equality, and solutions that take into account the particular difficulties marginalized women face must be developed. Real progress necessitates admitting that one-size-fits-all strategies frequently fail to protect the most vulnerable. For those who find themselves as "The First and Only," their journey is about transforming the spaces they step into. These women's stories show that intersectionality is about real experiences shaping careers, leadership paths, and opportunities.

Many women of colour carry the unseen weight of constant self-assessment, the need to demonstrate their worth, and are facing unspoken expectations. However, history tells us that there are women who don't just manage to get by—they thrive. They take on outdated power structures, forge new models of leadership, and redefine what's achievable for the generations that follow them.

What defines true leadership? Is it power, status, or the ability to make difficult choices for a greater good? Throughout history, leaders who have led with purpose tend to stand alone—facing opposition, criticism, and even hostility. But their vision, resolve, and persistence have reshaped industries, policies, and movements. In masculine settings, purposeful leadership is not a choice—it is a requirement to tear down barriers. This chapter explores women leaders who did not lead for themselves but for a higher purpose than themselves-to change societies in the bargain.

Purpose-driven leadership

Purposeful leadership is not just about personal ambition—it's about making a better tomorrow and bringing lasting change to society. To women breaking barriers in male-dominated professions, purpose gives guidance and empowerment. Their stories show that working for the greater good is more than an abstract ideal—it is a principle that shapes choices and drives impact. Questioning norms that limit possibilities is one of the identifying characteristics of purpose-driven leadership. Indian author, philanthropist, and chairperson of Infosys Foundation Sudha Murthy is a fine case in point. In her early years, she saw an ad for engineers at Tata Engineering and Locomotive Company (TELCO) declaring quite unapologetically, "Men only."

Instead of surrendering to defeat, she picked up a pen and wrote a letter to J.R.D. Tata, the head of the company. Her words weren't just a complaint—they were a challenge to a system built to exclude. To her surprise, Tata responded, and soon, Sudha Murthy became the first female engineer at TELCO. But that was not the end. Her male colleagues dismissed her, questioned her presence, and doubted her abilities at every turn. Yet, she refused to leave. She didn't just enter the room—she changed it.

Her success was not just a personal achievement. It reflected her deep belief in equal opportunities. This conviction continued to shape her leadership at the Infosys Foundation. Her purpose-driven leadership has transformed business culture. It has pulled many out of poverty and changed lives through a variety of initiatives. These initiatives have improved healthcare and education for underserved communities.

Leadership beyond Politics

Gro Harlem Brundtland, Norway's first female Prime Minister, is a good example of how leadership can extend beyond politics. She is known as the "mother of sustainable development", for a reason. Social equality and protecting the environment were very important to her. Her leadership in sustainability was not just theoretical—it was transformative. The Brundtland Report did more than introduce a concept; it redefined global policymaking. It formed the basis of the UN's Sustainable Development Goals (SDGs), influencing global agreements and climate and equality policy decades later. World leaders, from ministers to green campaigners, cite the Brundtland Report as a tipping point in the debate on sustainability.

Purpose-driven leadership often begins with a deep personal commitment to change. Ela Bhatt, an Indian cooperative organizer, and founder of Self-Employed Women's Association (SEWA), dedicated her life to empowering women through economic independence. Ela Bhatt once said, 'Poverty is not merely a lack of income. It is a lack of choices, opportunities, and dignity.' She did not just seek to uplift women economically—she sought to redefine their place in society. Under her leadership, SEWA became a lifeline for over two million women. These were women who were previously invisible in the economic life of India—domestic workers, textile workers, and street vendors. SEWA was a movement towards self-respect, economic empowerment, and collective voice for them, not just an organization.

Impact of Purpose-driven leadership

The impact of purpose-driven leadership reaches much beyond the leaders themselves. Women like Sudha Murthy, Gro Harlem Brundtland, and Ela Bhatt have inspired others to set goals and take charge. Their commitment has opened doors for future generations. They demonstrate that titles and honours are not what define leadership. It is about making a lasting difference and bringing hope. But having a purpose is not simple. Overcoming challenges and personal adversity requires a great deal of strength. The path may involve suffering, isolation, and betrayal. However, it's also a route of strength, change, and complete trust in the outcome. True purpose is tested in moments of doubt. Many purpose-driven leaders face rejection and loneliness before their impact is recognized. When Ela Bhatt started SEWA, she faced resistance from both business leaders and government officials who dismissed her vision. She was isolated from decision-making rooms, yet she persisted—knowing economic independence was the key to women's empowerment.

In male-dominated industries, leadership often requires not just skill but courage. Lise Klaveness, President of the Norwegian Football Federation, knows all about this. Lise walked onto the FIFA Congress stage in 2022 knowing exactly what she was about to do—challenge the very institution she was part of. The room was filled with some of the most powerful figures in global football, many of whom had spent years avoiding difficult conversations about human rights and discrimination. And then, she spoke. She didn't just deliver a speech—she shattered an unspoken rule of compliance. Her words cut through the room, demanding accountability, equality, and integrity in a sport that often resisted change.

Her speech resonated far beyond the conference room

"I stand here as Norway's first female football President, honoured to speak before you. I no longer carry a football everywhere, but my dreams remain the same. I dream of a game where boys and girls, people of all colors, straights and queers—everyone—is treated with equal respect and recognition."

"Dear President, Dear Congress—I am new here. The girl with the orange ball has come a long way from home. People often ask me what it's like to work in a man's world. I always say: I don't. I do not work in a man's world. Football belongs to all girls and boys everywhere."

Her words challenged outdated power structures and set a new precedent for accountability and inclusion in sports leadership. The criticism and resistance Lise faced, both from the public and within FIFA, highlights the struggles of purpose-driven leadership. Yet, like Sudha Murthy, Gro Harlem Brundtland, and Ela Bhatt, she showed that true leadership means standing firm despite challenges for the greater good. In 2022, for her fearless speech addressing human rights violations and discrimination at FIFA's International Congress in Qatar, Lise Klaveness was awarded the Freedom of Expression Foundation Tribute.

Lise's journey is a powerful example for future leaders. She proves that courage break barriers and drives change. Her story, and the stories of other pioneers, remind us that leadership is not about earning personal praise but about making lasting change that serves and inspires everyone.

Chapter 10
Mentorship and Allyship

Mentorship and allyship are key support networks. For women who are the "first and only" in their positions, these networks offer support, encouragement, and affiliation. Navigating the obstacles confronting them often involves emotional and workplace hurdles, and having mentors is helpful.

The Power of Mentorship

When women are down, they need a good role model to stand by them. Take the case of Priya Singh, a bright and hardworking engineer and the first female in her department in one of India's leading technology firms. Her male colleagues questioned her ability from the very first day. Not for anything she did, but just because she was a woman. She felt lonely in meetings and was met with a hostile work atmosphere. There were times she felt as though the isolation took away her own value.

Then she found a mentor—a woman who was further along in business and had grappled with the same problems. During the coffee breaks and free discussions, her mentor addressed her by telling her stories, giving wise advice, and reassuring Priya when things became difficult. Her single advice to Priya was especially crucial: "You don't have to prove your worth to anyone but yourself." Those words resonated deeply.

Through this support, Priya got her confidence back. She started to speak up in meetings and assert her ideas, and manage work situations better. Soon, she became a mentor, supporting other women who were struggling in the same way. The emotional support that comes with mentorship is one of its most significant benefits. Besides career direction, it provides validation, approval, and reassurance that a woman's value is not in the hands of others.

The Role of Allies

Besides mentors, allies, men and women alike, are also vital to establishing inclusive workplaces. An ally who supports a woman's idea in a meeting, fights for her promotion, or makes sure that she has a place at the table helps her advance her career. Shared experience builds strong connections, but allyship involves more than people who share experiences. Isabelle Ringnes, prominent Norwegian tech entrepreneur, explains how important it is to break through biases: "Studies show that women underestimate themselves, men underestimate women—and partly that women underestimate other women." This shows why mentorship and allyship are important—they change how people think about things and boost confidence. Being a good ally is not simply a matter of stating that you believe in gender equality. Action is necessary. Allies must call out inequity, amplify women's ideas in meetings, and create opportunities for them to lead.

Trailblazers Who Paved the Way

Radha Ramaswami Basu is a renowned technology leader and mentor. Radha was often the "first and only" woman in many spaces. Born in India, she was instrumental in developing Hewlett-Packard in India and went on to become Chairman and CEO of NASDAQ-listed Support.com. Her journey started in Chennai, where she grew up in an educated family. Her parents supported her, and she studied

Mathematics and Science, because she loved to solve problems. She was the only female student amidst 2,800 male students at the College of Engineering, Guindy. Instead of being perturbed, she became strong, made lifelong friendships, and excelled.

She earned her master's in Computer Science and Biomedical Engineering from USC and later joined HP Labs. She started HP's first software center at Bengaluru in 1985, the first for a large company in India. Her vision started India's IT revolution, making way for firms like Infosys and Wipro.

Radha's impact extended beyond corporate success. She started social entrepreneurship in 2005 with the co-founding of the Anudip Foundation to provide empowerment for impoverished youth, especially women. The initiative later set up iMerit Technology Services, which teaches rural and tribal youth to perform digital work. Today, iMerit is a leader in AI data solutions, serving Fortune 500 companies.

Building Inclusive Networks

Mentors and allies offer more than career guidance—they offer emotional stamina, validation, and a sense of belonging. Self-doubt is common in male-dominated professions, but robust networks help women see their own potential and capabilities. Good mentorship is about more than giving advice. It's a two-way transaction that benefits mentor and mentee alike. Mentors are gratified by the success of others, and mentees receive the experience and confidence to persevere through challenge. Similarly, good allyship is about more than just standing on the sidelines as a bystander. What it really means is actively advocating for gender equity. Allies build workplaces where women have a voice and are listened to.

The experiences of pioneers such as Priya and Radha illustrate how mentors and allies can make all the difference. Such relationships assist not just in career advancement but also provide women with the strength to overcome challenges, grow resilient, and fulfil their potential. In making our spaces inclusive, we are shaping a future in which women are not isolated but thrive on support and opportunities to succeed.

This chapter shows how important mentorship and allyship are for women. Later in this book, we will cite instances of men who have supported women to become successful. These men have amplified the voices of women, advocated for their growth, and sometimes stepped back and let women lead.

Chapter 11
Master Suppression Techniques

We all encounter master suppression techniques, with women often facing them more frequently than men. Social psychologist Berit Å documented five primary suppression methods used to silence and undermine individuals, particularly women in male-dominated fields.

Suppression Tactic	Description	Example	How to Counter
Making Someone Invisible	Exclusion by intentional avoidance, making individuals feel unimportant or unheard.	Malin Anderson, a Nordic entrepreneur, proposed a sustainable business idea in a board meeting, but her idea was ignored. A male colleague later repeated the same idea and received praise.	Speak up repeatedly and restate your point if ignored. Find allies who amplify your ideas. Keep records of your contributions.

Ridicule	Undermining someone through jokes, criticism, or casting doubt on their credibility.	Falguni Nayar, founder of Nykaa, was ridiculed when she left a banking career to start an online beauty business. Many doubted her, but she proved them wrong with a billion-dollar company.	Stay confident and do not internalize ridicule. Address inappropriate remarks directly. Prove your critics wrong with results.
Withholding Information	Excluding individuals from key discussions or emails, preventing them from making informed decisions.	Meera Kapoor, a talented software engineer, noticed she was left out of crucial project emails, making it difficult to contribute effectively. She proactively built relationships and raised the issue with management.	Ask questions and request important updates. Build relationships with key decision-makers. Keep track of exclusion and report if necessary.

Double Binding	*Creating a no-win situation where women are judged harshly regardless of their actions.*	*Annika Larson, a Nordic CEO, was called "too aggressive" when making firm decisions but "indecisive" when listening to feedback. She chose to focus on results rather than stereotypes.*	*Be yourself and focus on your goals. Reframe criticism into strengths. Accept useful feedback and ignore baseless judgments.*
Heaping Blame and Putting to Shame	*Unfairly blaming women for failures, even when decisions were collective.*	*Dr. Priya Jain, a professor, was blamed for financial issues in a study led by her team, even though budget decisions were made collectively. She defended herself with documented evidence.*	*Clarify roles and responsibilities. Use records and facts to defend yourself. Promote shared accountability in teams.*

Beyond Ås's five suppression techniques, women face additional challenges in professional settings. Tactics like exclusion from social networks, tokenism, and gaslighting reaffirm systemic obstacles too.

- Gaslighting makes a person question their own skills or what they see. This creates doubt and loss of confidence.

- Tokenism places undue pressure on a single woman to represent all women. This reinforces stereotypes and increases mistrust.

- Exclusion from casual networks, frequently regarded as "boys' clubs", prevents women from being involved in vital decision-making when key business discussions take place.

How to Develop Resilience and Allyship

While resilience is important, lasting change requires systemic solutions. Women in male-dominated fields can take proactive steps to counter suppression:

- *Establish Support Systems*: Build networks with other women to share strategies and experiences. Peer networks provide validation and collective strength.

- *Educate and Train*: Increase awareness within organizations. This helps to expose these tactics and mitigates their effects.

- *Involve Allies*: Engage male colleagues to advocate for inclusion. This promotes broader change.

Addressing these patterns starts with recognizing them. Then, the way forward is to form strong peer networks, raise organizational awareness, and enlist allies. Individual resilience is crucial, but real progress depends on collective action. Together, men and women can challenge discriminatory practices and create inclusive workplaces.

The Burden of Office Housework and Systemic Undermining in Leadership

Nina Hansen, a senior-level executive and the sole female on her management team, was repeatedly given work that hampered her career growth. Event planning and administrative duties took up her time and kept her from high-visibility projects essential for advancements. Research finds that female leaders are given non-promotable tasks.

Men do strategic work as women do logistical work, reinforcing gender stereotypes that dissuade career growth.

However, the challenges extend beyond workload allocation. Women in leadership often face deeper systemic barriers, including having their successes denied or undermined, regardless of their actual performance.

Despite exceeding all targets set by the executive leadership team, Nina was dismissed by a senior male colleague who argued that if she had met the targets, then they must have been set too low. Even after fulfilling every directive, leading an engaged team, and earning a full performance bonus, her achievements were downplayed. This was not just about workload—it was about reshaping reality to diminish her contributions.

To make matters worse, the same leader later claimed she had received a verbal warning—something she knew had never happened. When she requested access to her records, she confirmed that no such warning existed. Confronted with the facts, the leader was forced to retract his claim, but the damage had been done. The tactic of planting false doubts about her competence had succeeded in casting a shadow over her leadership.

The breaking point came during a meeting with three senior executives. Instead of discussing company performance, the conversation revolved around Nina's leadership suitability. She had exceeded expectations, successfully led a business transition, and had a satisfied and engaged team. Yet, the discussion centered not on her results, but on questioning whether she belonged in leadership. Finally, she asked a pointed question: "What do you think of your own leadership?" The room fell silent. Her lawyer cut through the tension with a blunt statement: "We need to find a solution. They don't want you here."

Nina's case illustrates the double bind women in leadership face. If they take on additional responsibilities and tolerate systemic biases, they reinforce expectations that these burdens belong to them. If they resist, they risk being labelled uncooperative. More alarmingly, their achievements can be rewritten to fit a narrative that excludes them from leadership roles altogether.

Understanding master suppression techniques is about equipping yourself with knowledge. Women can shatter these barriers with self-education, building effective networks, and creating welcoming workplaces. By becoming aware of these invisible barriers, resisting them, and changing them, we begin to open doors to rooms where all voices can be heard—and where leadership depends on ability, not gender.

Chapter 12
The Burden of Breaking Barriers

Breaking barriers is an impressive feat, but for women in male-dominated fields, it is can be at an emotional and social price. They might feel pressure to speak for their entire gender, withstand increased scrutiny, and manage cultural expectations. This pressure is crushing and it complicates leadership further. Women leaders feel they have to work twice as hard to be taken seriously. Emotional support networks in the workplace are still in short supply. This situation is a recipe for anxiety, self-doubt, and reluctance to take risks.

The Pressure of Representation

The fight for gender equality is deeply tied to the battle against the institutional barriers that keep inequality alive. Women who break these barriers tend to become icons of change. Whether or not they accept this status, their achievements are never regarded as personal. They are considered evidence of what all women can or cannot accomplish. If they succeed, they affirm women's capabilities. If they fail, it is inappropriately employed to undermine women's abilities.

Emotional Resilience in the Face of Criticism

Senior-level women, on average, report feeling even more stringent criticism. Research has indicated that female leaders receive more severe judgments than their male counterparts. For women in politics and executive positions, their assessment is frequently cantered on how they communicate, dress, and present themselves, not their work performance. A female CEO needs to appear strong without being seen as threatening and empathetic without appearing weak. These are mutually exclusive demands.

Isolation in Leadership

Being the sole woman in a leadership team or profession can be lonely. Lacking peers who comprehend their situation, most women cannot get support. Underrepresentation is not just about quantity—it has an impact on access to vital decision-making forums. Most informal networks, where actual decisions are made, are still male dominated. In finance, important discussions take place over golf games. In tech startups, bonds are formed over late-night cocktails. Women may not be included in these environments, restricting their influence and career advancement.

Emotional Cost of Breaking Barriers

Leadership involves strength and resilience. Women leaders repress emotions to prevent being termed "too emotional." They have to maintain confidence at all times, aware that showing frustration or doubt would reinforce gender stereotypes. As time passes, this suppressed emotion erodes confidence. Absent a healthy support network, self-advocacy grows more challenging. Isolation of leadership can manifest as burnout, self-doubt, and exhaustion. The relentless scrutiny leaves its mark. The pressure to be perfect discourages risk-taking and hinders personal growth. Years of fighting for a seat at the table causes chronic stress, guilt, and a sense of never being fully present in either professional or personal life.

The Fear of Failure and Its Consequences

Failure is a part of leadership, but for women, its consequences are amplified. If a male leader fails, it is viewed as a one-off mistake. But if a woman pioneer fails, it is used to validate scepticism regarding women's ability to lead.

This fear of failure can cause reluctance to take bold action. A woman executive may hesitate to pursue a risky innovation, worrying that failure would perpetuate negative stereotypes. This cycle restricts opportunities for growth and strengthens a culture in which women feel they have to be perfect in order to succeed.

Female leaders who fight hard to gain new rights for themselves and for all women often have to fight just as hard to get their business ideas accepted. A 'first and only' who has succeeded in becoming a leader is likely to be strong, self-confident, and capable of execution. Confidence is essential, but so is the ability to collaborate and recognize the value of surrounding oneself with other strong individuals who can provide professional pushback. The goal is to refine the edges of a business idea until it becomes as feasible as possible before being introduced to the real world. In this way, a 'first and only' leader can more effectively reach the company's business objectives — and, through that, build a foundation for gaining recognition and advancing women's rights. On the flip side, it can be easy to be pushed out of a leadership role if a 'first and only' becomes too independent and fails to see the value of shaping business ideas with input from others before putting them into practice.

Indra Nooyi in her book, '*My Life in Full: Work, Family, and Our Future*', adds another twist. Women are still required to be chief caregivers and feel guilty when they put their careers first. A male businessman putting in overtime is admired for his commitment, but a woman doing the same will be scolded for abandoning her family. These double standards can create deep emotional tension.

Breaking Barriers, Bearing the Burden

Skarstein, six-time World Champion rower and Nordic skier, knows this burden all too well. Paralympic champion and Norway's top adaptive sportsperson, she has won considerable success in her sport while advocating for the visibility and inclusion of para-athletes. Her own success draws attention as well as significant responsibility. Even as a star athlete, Skarstein encountered barriers not because of her performance but because of institutional red tape. Before the Paralympic Games, she was locked out of Norway's para-ski team by an administrative row between the nation's rowing and skiing federations. It was a shattering experience. She wondered if the price—months and months of training alone and mental toughness—had been too steep. Without a network, she had to find the logistics of her training on her own, something no other elite-level athlete in her situation would ever have to do.

Skarstein realized that success and failure on all occasions would be attributed to her not simply as an individual but as characteristic of para-athletes everywhere. The fact that she alone would bear that weight made failing more difficult. Instead of drawing back, though, she rode out the defeat in order to stir her fire anew, driven ever forward, no matter that chances often seemed stacked against her.

Skarstein's tale is one of unrelenting grit, but it also highlights the unspoken emotional cost of shattering barriers. Even after her success, the journey has been lonely and draining. But she keeps pushing forward, aware that each struggle she wages makes the way a little less difficult for the women who will follow her.

Elite sport requires long periods of training in isolation from family, friends and familiar surroundings. While solitude suits some athletes, others find the long-term loneliness challenging. For women like Skarstein, success and failure on all occasions would be attributed to them not simply as individuals but as characteristic of women everywhere. Despite this harsh reality, Skarstein continued to compete and show up on the global stage, setting a stellar example not just for paralympic sportswomen but for women all over the world.

Part 3

Chapter 13
Leading with Purpose

Leadership is often associated with power, authority, and influence, but for those who are the first and only in their fields, it also comes with challenges that go beyond professional expertise. Women who break barriers in male-dominated industries, entrepreneurship, and social impact not only redefine success for themselves but also create lasting change for others.

This section highlights the journeys of five remarkable leaders: Anette Holte, Anna Wagner Norseng, Kristin Andresen, Vidya Basarkod, and Ajaita Shah. Each has taken bold strides in different industries while navigating cultural, societal, and structural challenges. Their stories showcase how resilience, adaptability, and vision drive transformation, not just in their careers but across industries and communities.

Anette Holte has forged a path in the maritime and engineering industry, a sector traditionally dominated by men. As Country Manager for Kongsberg Maritime India, she has redefined leadership by bridging Norwegian and Indian business cultures, fostering gender diversity, and championing inclusive policies that make workplaces more equitable.

Anna Wagner Norseng has established a thriving import business, often being the only woman in male-dominated negotiations in India. She has had to assert her presence to earn respect in a sector where decision-making is typically dominated by men. Through strategic relationship-building, she has not only navigated cultural and gender biases but has also educated her suppliers on gender equality, demonstrating that strong leadership transcends barriers.

Kristin Andresen, an entrepreneur and social innovator, has worked at the grassroots level in Rajasthan, India, empowering women through education, financial independence, and sustainable community projects. Her journey highlights how long-term commitment and cultural understanding can transform entire villages and create opportunities where they once seemed impossible.

Vidya Basarkod, an engineering leader with decades of experience in India and Scandinavia, has not only shattered glass ceilings in infrastructure and technology but has also led the shift toward more diverse and inclusive leadership models in global organizations.[110] Her insights on Nordic vs. Indian leadership styles reveal key lessons in balancing structure with flexibility and vision with execution.

Ajaita Shah is revolutionizing rural commerce and women's economic empowerment through her social enterprise, Frontier Markets. By leveraging technology, she has built a network of thousands of rural women entrepreneurs, proving that women are not just beneficiaries of change but the architects of a new, inclusive economy. What unites these women is their ability to challenge deep-seated biases—whether in corporate boardrooms, remote villages, or competitive industries—and their relentless pursuit of equity, sustainability, and social impact.

As you read through this section, consider how these leaders adapt to different cultural landscapes, overcome resistance, proving that strong leadership transcends barriers. Their experiences are not just stories of personal triumph; they offer lessons in leadership, purpose-driven innovation, and the power of breaking barriers for future generations.

Chapter 14

Annette Holte on Paving the Way as the First

Traditionally controlled by men, leadership demands determination, vision, and an emphasis on inclusion. Kongsberg Maritime India's Country Manager, Annette Holte, exhibits these traits. She has an outstanding record and has been a vocal supporter of diversity. She has effectively led the company in India's intricate and rapidly evolving market as a leader at one of Norway's leading maritime technology companies. She has maintained high standards while adapting the company's ethics and ideals to the local business environment.

Her leadership has not only increased the company's visibility in India but also acted as an example for other female employees in the industry. Her behaviour proves that knowledge, adaptability, and a commitment to positive change are all critical elements of successful leadership. Through perseverance and hard work, Holte has established a solid career since joining Kongsberg Maritime in 2007. She is constantly willing to pick up new skills, adjust, and take on new tasks. Her leadership style and global perspective have been shaped by her experiences in Saudi Arabia and San Francisco. Because of her experiences, she has been able to traverse many marketplaces and lead with confidence.

As she travels across countries, Holte has a high respect for cultural diversity. As she lives and works in different environments she has developed an understanding of multiple viewpoints. This has made her a successful leader in the corporate world.[108] She has developed the ability to modify her strategy in accordance with cultural norms. This enables her to establish trusting bonds and promote cooperation. Her leadership style has also been impacted by her international exposure. She ensures that decisions are both locally relevant and globally informed by fusing local company strategy with global insights. One of her greatest professional strengths has been her capacity to cross cultural divides.

Life's important lessons

Finding a balance between efficiency and empathy is one of the most important lessons she has learned. She leads with empathy and decisiveness because she recognizes the importance of people to a business's success. She has led diverse teams, effectively navigated challenging marketplaces, and sparked significant change within her organization with her approach. Her leadership style combines strategic thought, cultural intelligence, and flexibility. Holte is a trailblazer who promotes inclusive leadership in the marine business, thanks to her ability to lead in a variety of settings. She saw an opportunity to move her career on a fresh and interesting path when it presented itself inside Kongsberg Maritime's operations in India.[108] Instead of hesitating at the difficulties of relocating abroad, she confidently seized the chance.

India's rapidly growing economy and her strong maritime ties with Norway made the move even more appealing. She saw the potential to grow in a dynamic market. She even viewed this transition as a chance to apply her global expertise in a fresh setting. She remained determined to make an impact despite the complexities of entering a new market. Holte's choice shows her belief that opportunities should be grabbed instead of waiting for the right moment. Her success in India's fast-paced marine industry has largely been attributed to her capacity for change management, environmental adaptation, and resilient leadership.

Annette Holte's move to Mumbai was both a thrilling and difficult experience. The city was a sharp contrast to Norway. Norway has a population of just over 5 million people and is a peaceful and orderly place, compared to Mumbai which had 25 million people and a fast-paced vitality.[108] She was not familiar with the busy streets, congested marketplaces, and fast-paced corporate environment. Though the shift brought many chances for both professional and personal development, it also came with certain difficulties.

Recognizing the nuances of Indian culture at work was one of the most difficult changes. She wasn't used to how people in the corporate world communicated, made choices, and cultivated relationships. She had to learn by doing simple things like grocery shopping and negotiating the unwritten laws of social relationships. More significantly, she had to put in more effort to build credibility and adjust to a new leadership style because she was a foreigner and a woman in a male-dominated field.

Every element of day-to-day existence had to be reconstructed. Holte, however, welcomed the event as a worthwhile educational opportunity rather than viewing it as a negative. She relied on her staff of 150 workers, realizing that humility, flexibility, and teamwork were necessary for effective leadership in a new setting.[102] She not only adapted but flourished over time, transforming her initial uneasiness into a profound admiration for India's dynamic business environment and lively culture.

Stepping into the unknown

The feeling of being "thrown into the dark" was exhausting at times. An important factor in Annette Holte's effortless transfer into her new position in India was her team. They were her staunchest supporters from the start, helping her manage cultural and professional challenges. Their cooperation and trust gave her a solid platform on which to successfully combine Indian workplace culture with Norwegian leadership ideals.

Annette spent time observing, listening, and learning from her coworkers instead of enforcing a strict leadership approach. She understood that desire, perseverance, and hard effort are fundamental to Indian workplace culture. She greatly loved the exceptional flexibility and commitment that employees frequently showed. Adopting these principles allowed her to improve her approach to leadership, ensuring that it resonated with her team.

She created a work climate that encouraged creativity, inclusivity, and progress for everyone. She skilfully fused the most effective of the two worlds—Norwegian efficiency and Indian tenacity. She did it through open communication and respect for one another. Annette soon discovered that the work culture in India differed greatly from the Norwegian one she was used to.

Competition is an important factor in Indian companies. This frequently functions under a hierarchical framework with centralized decision-making. Workers typically respect authority figures. They adhere to established procedures, which fosters a disciplined and structured work atmosphere.

On the other hand, Norwegian organizations emphasise flat hierarchies and open and direct communication. It is more collaborative leadership. There is a higher sense of autonomy and inclusivity. The employees are encouraged to exchange their ideas freely and decision-making is frequently delegated. Understanding these distinctions, Annette modified her management style to combine the two methods. She respected India's organized and aspirational work culture while upholding the Norwegian values of openness and inclusivity. Her talent in uniting different professional opinions became her most important strength. She achieved operational effectiveness by uniting both performance standards with adaptable practices thus creating a workplace environment that empowered and directed the workforce until the company succeeded.

Being a woman in the male-dominated maritime industry, Annette experienced firsthand the obstacles women encounter at work. Her leadership style at Kongsberg Maritime India involved two main priorities: expansion of their business and working towards creating the perfect environment for inclusivity. From her personal encounters, she deduced that establishing opportunities and supplying necessary tools were vital for women who sought success in the industry.

The main difficulty encountered by many Indian women exists in their struggle to return to work after childbirth. Gender diversity in the sector is greatly impacted by the fact that cultural expectations and a lack of workplace flexibility sometimes cause women to permanently leave their employment.

Annette fought for laws that promoted a better work-life balance in order to remedy this. She made it simpler for women to balance work and family obligations. She introduced flexible work schedules and a hybrid work setting. She also emphasized the need for strong parental leave laws to help employees, both men and women, feel supported in balancing work and personal commitments. She established a new benchmark for diversity in the marine sector and advanced gender parity through these initiatives.

Promoting Inclusion at Work

Annette Holte understood that action was needed to create a truly inclusive workplace, not just policies. Many corporations view the legal requirement for crèche facilities for companies with more over 50 employees in India as merely a compliance measure rather than a chance for good change. But Holte had a different take on it. She fully embraced the rule, making sure Kongsberg Maritime India established a workplace that encouraged parents, especially moms. Employees were able to bring their kids to work thanks to the company's on-site childcare, which lessened the strain of juggling work and family obligations. This program promoted a culture in which both parents may actively participate in childcare duties in addition to encouraging women to return to the workforce.

Beyond this, Annette made important efforts to integrate inclusion and diversity into the organization's very foundation. She performed awareness training to combat biases, established fair recruitment procedures to guarantee equal opportunities, and launched mentorship programs to assist professional advancement. Her stance was unambiguous: diversity required concrete, quantifiable acts; it could not only be a theoretical idea. According to her, in order for an organization to truly be inclusive, it must actively put rules in place that level the playing field and go beyond rhetoric. Kongsberg Maritime India rose to prominence as a model for gender diversity in the maritime sector under her direction. In addition to empowering women, she established a standard for other businesses to follow by making structural reforms a top priority. Her initiatives proved that creating an inclusive workplace is advantageous to all parties involved, resulting in increased creativity, engagement, and long-term success.

Breaking Boundaries in the Maritime Sector

In India and around the world, the maritime sector has historically been controlled by men, with few opportunities for women to hold technical or leadership positions. But Annette Holte was determined to alter that story. At Kongsberg Maritime India, she and her colleagues took decisive action to question established conventions and establish a more inclusive and varied workplace. Under her direction, the APAC region's first female mechanical service engineer was hired, marking one of the most significant turning points. There were difficulties with this choice. The role's physical demands and harsh surroundings raised many questions about whether a woman could handle them. Fairness issues arose because of deep-rooted industrial biases rather than because of ability.

A major hiring manager decided to proceed in spite of these reservations, motivated by the idea of a time when his own daughter would be free to follow any vocation. In addition to providing opportunities for women in technical positions, this crucial choice established a solid standard inside the company. It made it very evident that opportunities should be determined by aptitude and talent rather than gender. This change was mostly driven by Annette's leadership. She made sure that Kongsberg Maritime India became an environment where women felt strong and supported by actively supporting diversity efforts. The company's dedication to breaking down barriers was demonstrated by its receipt of the renowned National Diversity Impact Award, which brought national exposure to her efforts.

This initiative's success extended beyond just one hire. It prompted other businesses in the sector to reconsider their hiring procedures and spurred more women to enter careers that have historically been filled by men. Through her work, Annette showed that diversity is about building a culture in which all people, regardless of gender, have the chance to succeed rather than merely focusing on representation.

By using Annette Holte as a role model in its diversity projects and recruitment strategies, Kongsberg Maritime India made a strong statement about equality and inclusivity. Her leadership style is based on open communication, trust, and collaboration, all of which she actively fosters in her team. In competitive environments, information is often seen as a source of power, leading to segmented decision-making.

Annette, though, adopted a different strategy. She made sure that her team worked with mutual trust rather than secrecy by promoting openness and knowledge exchange. She intentionally communicated excessively to establish an example of openness for her team, in addition to keeping everyone informed. By doing this, she created a work atmosphere where employees felt valued, heard, and inspired to contribute.

Annette Holte's leadership style was greatly influenced by Scandinavian principles, which place a strong emphasis on equality, trust, and a flat organizational structure. These values ran counter to the hierarchical structure of Indian companies, where decisions are often influenced by seniority and power.[102] But instead of enforcing a completely alien leadership model, she deftly modified her approach to overcome the cultural divide. She rapidly gained her employees' trust by acting in a straightforward, honest, and consistent manner. Her leadership style focused on showcasing the advantages of change through routine procedures rather than imposing it suddenly. She set an example by promoting candid communication, appreciating opinions from all levels, and making sure each worker felt heard.

She is "a unique blend of clear direction and a feminine touch," according to the HR chief. Because of this mix, she was able to create an atmosphere at work where everyone, regardless of status or background, felt appreciated and empowered. Her leadership in India was distinguished by her capacity to change without sacrificing her moral principles.

Promoting Gender Diversity in a Sustainable Way

Kongsberg Maritime India's dedication to gender diversity is backed up by tangible, significant measures rather than just declarations of purpose. Understanding that systemic support is necessary for true inclusivity, the organization has taken a number of steps to provide a safe and empowering work environment for women. These include free sanitary pad distribution, full health benefits, and self-defence education programs aimed at boosting women's self-esteem and safety.

However, encouraging gender diversity requires more than just helping women; it also entails actively enlisting males as supporters. Diversity and inclusion are important elements of the organization's leadership development programs, which make sure that individuals in charge of making decisions are aware of their responsibility to promote an egalitarian workplace. By including males in these programs, the business developed male diversity ambassadors and made gender inclusion a shared duty rather than a problem that just affected women.

Annette Holte stressed the importance of quantifiable results in order to promote long-term transformation. She established explicit diversity-related KPIs and connected them to performance rewards like bonus plans. In order to ensure that gender balance remained a strategic focus rather than merely a corporate value statement, the company established a culture of accountability by linking diversity targets to concrete rewards.[108] Her leadership demonstrated that sustained gender diversity requires shared commitment, cultural change, and regular action at all organizational levels rather than sporadic initiatives.

Throughout her time in India, Annette Holte's goal is to establish an environment at work that promotes equality and long-term inclusivity for all. According to her, diversity needs to be a fundamental part of an organization's culture rather than a short-term endeavour.[102] Her leadership in India, where she has effectively assembled a team with equal representation of the sexes, is evidence of this vision.

Gender diversity at Kongsberg Maritime India has advanced significantly under her direction. The company has seen a 33% increase in the number of women working there over the last five years, demonstrating that steady attention and well-designed policies can result in quantifiable change. This accomplishment demonstrates the company's dedication to breaking down boundaries and goes beyond a simple number.

Maintaining this momentum in the future is part of Annette's plan, which calls for ongoing policy improvements, assistance for women's career advancement, and the creation of an atmosphere where genius flourishes regardless of gender. She is adamant that diversity is about fostering a culture in which men and women feel heard, respected, and equipped to achieve, not just about numbers. She wants to leave a legacy of diversity that shapes the organization for years to come by laying a solid foundation today.

Chapter 15

Kristin Andresen on Women-Led Development

Kristin Andresen is a well-known Norwegian entrepreneur who has been working to empower women in India for over 20 years. Her journey started through her family company, FERD, which supported Base Camp Explorer's projects in Africa. Thanks to her friend, Svein Wilhelmsen, who led these efforts in Masai Mara, she became deeply inspired by the work they were doing for community development, especially for women. She wanted to contribute in a place where she could make a bigger impact.

Svein once shared an interesting idea with her. He had met an Indian man, Pradhuman Singh, at a tourism fair. Singh was from a small village in Rajasthan and wanted to turn his ancestral haveli (a small castle) into a hotel. He also aimed to start projects that would benefit the local villages. Rajasthan, with its rich culture, also had many areas struggling with poverty. Singh's vision to uplift his community caught Kristin's interest. Svein encouraged her to meet him. Trusting Svein's judgment, she decided to visit India. She had never been in the country before and was unsure of what to expect.

She went to the Rajasthani village of Chandelao after reaching Jodhpur. Despite the difficult trek, she welcomed the novel experience. She had never met Pradhuman Singh before. She didn't know much about Rajasthan's challenges. She had no clear plan except to meet him. But she trusted her instincts. Svein believed in Singh's vision, so she wanted to explore it too. Singh welcomed her warmly. He shared his idea of starting an arts and crafts centre. His goal was to create jobs for local women. But he didn't have the money to make it happen.

At that time, Base Camp planned to shift focus back to Africa. They asked her to take responsibility for the project. Singh became her partner, and they started reworking the plans. At first, the idea seemed too small. If they wanted to help more women, they had to think bigger. So, they expanded the project to create more jobs and have a greater impact. The initiative was run through Singh's foundation. Neither of them took a salary. They did this work because they believed in it. She took on this work independently. She didn't have a big organization or team to support her. She used her own resources and made decisions on her own. This gave her the freedom to learn and grow in new ways.

From Arts and Crafts to Education: Empowering Village Women

For her project, she worked closely with Mr. Singh and the village council. The council represented three villages, including Chandelao. They helped identify the community's needs and shape the project. But her main focus was always on empowering women. When they started the arts and crafts center, she faced a surprising challenge. None of the 35 women they hired could read or write. She found this hard to believe. She wanted to understand why. She visited local schools to find answers. What she discovered was even more shocking. Not a single girl had studied beyond the sixth grade. Social norms were the reason. She knew she had to do something to help keep girls in school.

At first, she thought about starting a foundation. She considered giving parents financial help, like paying for school fees and uniforms. But something didn't feel right. She wanted to hear directly from the parents.

With a translator's help, she visited families with daughters in sixth grade. She asked them why they didn't send their girls to school. The problem wasn't money—it was safety. The school was in the next village, and the girls had to walk there. Parents feared they might be harassed on the way. In their culture, such incidents could bring shame to the family. A girl facing trouble could become a burden instead of an asset. This was the real reason girls weren't going to school. She wouldn't have understood this without talking to the families herself. The solution was simple but effective. She suggested buying a school bus and hiring a driver. This would safely take the girls to school and back home.

The parents quickly agreed. The impact was immediate. Girls who had been stuck at home started going to school. Many later went to college and university. This proved that solutions don't always have to be expensive or complicated. The arts and crafts centre also grew over time. The younger women who joined had a better education than before. The older women also started learning. They attended daily classes along with their work.

At first, she suggested keeping the centre open longer for lessons. But their husbands objected. So, they changed the schedule. They included lessons during regular work hours. This way, the women could learn without facing trouble at home. Watching them learn to read and write was a joy. Their pride in their new skills was clear. Whenever she visits, they read to her or write letters as a thank-you.

One moment was especially touching. She asked some women why learning to read and write was so important to them. They gave a simple answer. They wanted to be able to write their husbands' names. This small step gave them hope. It showed that education does more than change minds. It also strengthens relationships and self-worth.

Transforming Schools and Breaking Taboos

There are many barriers to women's empowerment in this region. One major issue was menstrual hygiene. Kristin worked on a project to discuss menstrual hygiene in schools. She included both girls' schools and co-ed institutions. "It was common for girls to miss a week of school every month because of their periods. There were no proper toilets or sanitation facilities. This meant they lost nearly a fourth of their school days," she explained.

To solve this, Kristin and her team built toilets in public schools. "This simple step made a big difference. Girls could now attend school regularly without discomfort or embarrassment." They also added kitchens and dining areas. "At least one hot meal a day ensured students had the energy to focus on learning," she said. Though these changes were basic, they had a huge impact on attendance and overall well-being.

She also highlighted another major challenge—absent teachers. "The poor quality of education discourages parents from sending their children to school," she said. Overcrowding made things worse. "Some classrooms have 30 to 40 children sitting on the floor with no proper ventilation," she added. This makes learning difficult. The only solution is to improve school infrastructure.

Expanding schools and raising teachers' salaries are the next steps to improving the education system.

Wilhelm von Geijer, Kristin's son, has been part of this effort for years. He teaches at the Computerized Learning Center and also works at the hotel. His commitment to the community is inspiring. Wilhelm's friend, Norwegian influencer Isabel Raad, visited Chandelao with Kristin. She generously donated money for a new school building. She also noticed that the children had no toys. In response, she bought out an entire toy store in Jodhpur. Distributing the toys to the children, local kindergartens, and schools was a heartwarming moment.

Building Economic Opportunities and Greener Communities

Water scarcity is another serious issue in Rajasthan that Kristin has worked on. The solution lies in collecting rainwater from the roofs, building water reservoirs and using rainwater harvesting. Kristin's tree planting project has stopped the spread of desert conditions and has improved the conditions for insects, birds and wildlife.

The village water reservoir has also been extended with higher walls and dikes leading more water into the reservoir. She loves visiting the lake and the extended forest they have developed. Wildlife and birds have returned. Tourists now enjoy birdwatching in the new forest, bringing life back to the area.

One of their tech initiatives was providing solar kits to women. These kits were designed so that women could assemble them at home and rent them out for extra income. Each kit included an outlet and two light bulbs, which were in high demand in the desert region.

Kristin Andresen has also built a computerized learning center for village school children. In the afternoons, youth and other villagers can attend lessons or qualify for the Indian Government Certificate. This certificate is free for girls, but boys must pay a small fee.[103] Unfortunately, many parents are unwilling to pay for their daughters' education. Kristin acknowledges that not all projects have gone as planned. Some failed, while others exceeded expectations. Girls who once could not attend school are now pursuing higher education. Seeing their pride in learning keeps her motivated. Every success, regardless of size, serves as a reminder of the significance of her work.

In addition to solving current issues, long-term reform is the aim. The community as a whole gains when women are empowered through economic and educational possibilities. Future generations benefit from ending the cycle of poverty. This journey has taught her to adapt, keep going, and stay committed, even when facing setbacks. Because of the community's adaptability and thankfulness, every obstacle is worthwhile.

Kristin's efforts support Shri Narendra Modi's goal of empowering, educating, protecting, and nurturing girls. Her projects focus on women's education and economic independence in Chandelao. These efforts have not only changed individual lives but also transformed the entire community. They serve as a model for sustainable development that others can follow. When discussing the effects of these initiatives, Kristin remarked, "What we see is remarkable. Chandelao and the surrounding environs have been transformed from some of Rajasthan's poorest villages to some of its most prosperous. Every time I go, I get to see this transition, which is immensely satisfying."

She also highlighted how different initiatives have created positive ripple effects. One such change was the conversion and expansion of the village's haveli (small castle) into a boutique hotel. This project has contributed to the area's growth and provided new economic opportunities for the people. Kristin explained that the hotel now has 22 double rooms and attracts a steady stream of tourists. "This brings income not just to the hotel but also to the arts and crafts center," she said. "Women create products that tourists love to buy." While most of the hotel staff are men, which is common in India, some women have started working in cleaning roles. "It's a small step, but it's progress," she added.

Kristin visits India twice a year, staying for about ten days each time. Each visit brings new developments. "India is changing so fast—it's like a rocket. Every six months, the village looks different. Twenty years ago, it was all camels and ox carts. Now, there are motorbikes, cars, and buses. Dirt tracks have turned into proper roads, and homes are cleaner and better maintained." She noted that plastic waste is still a problem, but overall, the village is much cleaner than before.

One cultural shift stood out to her. "When families earn money, their first priority is often building temples. These aren't small structures—they are grand marble temples. It's different from what I'm used to, but I respect that it's their way of expressing gratitude and prosperity."

Kristin's latest project focuses on supporting girls after marriage. "In Rajasthan, girls marry into another village and family within their caste. Although the caste system is officially abolished, it still exists in practice. When a girl marries, she often becomes the lowest-ranked member of her new family. She is usually not allowed to work outside the home."

To address this, Kristin is establishing a tailoring school. "We already have a tailoring department at the arts and crafts center, so this felt like a natural step. The goal is to train girls to become skilled tailors before they marry." Thanks to support from Sofie Beck and her expat friends, each girl receives a sewing machine as a wedding gift. "This allows her to work from home, take on clients, and even continue making products for our shop and online store. It's a way for her to contribute financially while gaining more respect within her family."

When asked about her message to the world, Kristin said, "There is poverty everywhere, and we all have a role to play. If each person does a little, together we can make a big difference. Businesses, in particular, can help empower women. Support must come from the top, but education is the foundation. It is the single most important factor in bringing social change."

Kristin pointed out the vast difference between urban and rural India. "In cities, progress for women is happening quickly. But in villages, where most of India's 1.3 billion people live, traditions still dominate. It often feels like stepping back into the 18th century. That's why education is so important in these areas. It is the key to changing mindsets and breaking cycles of poverty." She believes that empowering women in rural areas has a much wider impact. "Education promotes gender equality and helps women become part of the global economy. India is so diverse that you can't generalize, but in cities, you see women excelling in universities and leading global companies. There is huge potential here."

Kristin also sees opportunities for foreign companies to invest in India. "When international businesses support women, they can expand this impact on a much larger scale. The Indian government has made women's empowerment a priority, as seen in platforms like the World Economic Forum. With diversity, inclusivity, and the world's youngest population, India offers incredible potential."

Thinking back on her experiences in India, Kristin laughed about a question she often gets asked: "Where is your husband?" Her usual response is, "He's home looking after the children." She enjoys seeing the surprise on people's faces. "They look at me like I've said something outrageous. But maybe, seeing a woman working independently and making a difference plants a small seed of possibility. Maybe it makes them think, 'If she can do it, so can I.'"

Kristin's work has also revealed deeper cultural and systemic challenges. She shared an unexpected issue she faced with a solar kit project. "We gave women solar kits to assemble and rent out. These kits had an outlet and two lightbulbs, which were in high demand in the desert. The women did an excellent job assembling and renting them, but when it was time to collect payments, the men refused to pay. Husbands would disappear whenever the women came to collect their money."

Over time, the women grew frustrated. They had to walk long distances under the hot desert sun, only to return empty-handed. Eventually, they gave up, and the project had to be abandoned. "It was disappointing," Kristin admitted. "But even when a project fails, we learn valuable lessons. And those lessons help us find better ways to create change."

Lessons in Listening and the Power of Local Wisdom

Kristin's success comes from her focus on practical solutions and her willingness to adapt. "When I first started, I had no idea how much I would learn—not just about India, but about development work itself," she reflected. She realized that real solutions come from listening. "Many of the best ideas don't come from outsiders. They come from the community itself. My job is to listen and support what they truly need." Kristin admits that many of her ideas from Oslo did not always work well in India. "My 'office' solutions often turned out to be 'not a good idea' in reality," she said with a laugh. But now, she has a new project in mind—bringing a soft plastic collection initiative from Africa to India.

For eight years, she served on the advisory board of the Strøm Foundation, where she learned about a successful recycling project in Eastern Africa. There, soft plastic was collected and turned into school benches and desks. Inspired by this, Kristin hopes to start a similar project in India. "I have some great friends in Oslo with connections in the recycling industry. Maybe we can succeed in cleaning up the three villages—or even more," she said with optimism.

Kristin feels hopeful about the future. "When women have better education and work opportunities, the whole community benefits," she said. She believes in creating lasting change, not just solving immediate problems.

Every small step forward—whether a woman learning to read, signing her name for the first time, or a girl going to college—is proof of why this work matters. Kristin's journey in Rajasthan is a powerful example of what can happen when persistence meets cultural understanding. Her efforts show that even small actions, driven by dedication, can create lasting change despite deep-rooted traditions and challenges.

Chapter 16

Ajaita Shah's Vision for a 100-Million-Woman Economy

As the Founder and CEO of Frontier Markets, Ajaita Shah leads operations that unite rural households with crucial product and service purchases in India through her innovative AI-enabled social commerce platform, Meri Saheli App. The platform uses basic smartphone functions to enable women business owners to elevate and diversify their incomes by serving household needs in their local rural communities. Frontier Markets aims to impact 100 million rural women business owners through its mission by 2030.

Ajaita has maintained 20 years of experience across microfinance and rural distribution while developing gender-inclusive business strategies for rural women in India.[111] She has established both the Frontier Innovations Foundation (US 501c3 Foundation) and She-Leads Bharat (a global coalition of partners) which unite markets with local communities and government entities to drive climate-friendly and financial empowerment and health services through 100 million rural women. Through her work, she holds strong that rural women possess the capacity to both receive aid and lead transformative change processes.

Global Recognition and Grassroots Change

Through her contributions, Ajaita has established an international standing of recognition. As a winner of the Schwab Foundation Award for Social Entrepreneurship she is currently the sole Southeast Asian member of the UN Trade Advisory Council. Her path which began in Jaipur and led to global recognition has been exceptionally motivating. She was also handpicked and recognised by the honourable Prime Minister of India, Shri Narendra Modi on International Women's Day on 5th March 2025, where she took over his X (previously Twitter) handle to share about her journey and showcase the impact of this work in the lives of rural women.

Her mission centers on enhancing life quality for India's 800 million rural population. Real and sustained change becomes possible when resources go toward supporting women according to her viewpoint. Through Frontier Markets, she demonstrates that rural women as the locals understand their communities best, possess both natural leadership talents and problematic-solving abilities. Frontier Markets gave digital tools and skills together with smartphones and internet access to 35,000 Sahelis (digitally empowered women business owners) and enabled them to deliver over 100 million essential products and services to over 4 million rural customers in 3 states of India. Through their business activities, these women elevate their incomes and obtain data which companies convert into improved product offerings. The effective power of Frontier Markets results from uniting powerful data analytics with connectivity relationships and local trust structures to transform rural India through substantial changes.

Ajaita's journey has not been easy. As a 25-year-old with a New York accent, convincing people of her vision for rural India was a challenge. Many were skeptical, but her background in microfinance helped her prove her dedication. A major breakthrough came during demonetization when Frontier Markets quickly adapted to customer needs and became profitable. Over time, Ajaita has shown that rural India is not just a difficult market but a massive opportunity. This accomplishment has been made possible in large part by technology. Ajaita and her team collaborated extensively with rural women to create a platform that met their requirements as smartphones became more widely available. They can gather information, exchange ideas, and provide necessary services with the use of this digital instrument. Frontier marketplaces has uncovered the latent potential of rural marketplaces by fusing technology with their strong ties to the community.

Ajaita's strategy is centered on teamwork. She thinks that these issues cannot be resolved by a single group. In order to achieve the common objective of strengthening rural India, she envisions a system in which governments, corporations, and non-governmental organizations all make unique contributions.

Women continue to be central to her agenda above everything else. The Sahilis have done more than just promote girls' education and empowerment; they have stopped almost 200,000 child marriages. They are changing social norms from the inside out, demonstrating that supporting women has a long-lasting impact on communities and families.

Ajaita's path serves as a potent illustration of fortitude and vision. She is motivated by the perseverance, fortitude, and tenacity of the people she works with. These women are leaders bringing about genuine change in their communities, not only recipients of help. Even though Ajaita has accomplished a lot, she thinks much more has to be done. The future and the part these women will play in influencing it fascinate her.

Rooted in Two Worlds: A Childhood of Dual Identities

Although her family is originally from Jaipur, Rajasthan, Ajaita Shah was born in the United States. They practice Jainism and work as jewelers. Her childhood was influenced by this background in a special way. Her home life was very Indian, despite the fact that she was raised in New York. By the age of seven, she was proficient in reading, writing, and speaking Hindi. She prepared tea, studied Kathak, and enthusiastically celebrated holidays like Diwali. She was also impacted by American culture. She experienced both the fast-paced, international mentality of the US and traditional Indian beliefs, balancing both worlds. She was frequently called an "ABCD" (American Born Confused Desi) due to her strong ties to Indian customs while also living as an American.

She grew up in the 1980s and 1990s, when the US was at the forefront of international projects, collaborating with institutions like the UN and lending support to nations like Rwanda. Observing these initiatives caused her to reflect on her responsibilities as a responsible citizen and the state of the world. Later, she investigated how to combine these two worlds while attending Tufts University in Boston. She was looking for methods to change the world and learn more about her Indian heritage. She eventually came to the realization that she wanted to do something about the issues, not merely watch them unfold. It became evident that she was destined to work toward change, even though she is unable to identify the precise cause of this drive.

Ajaita tried to figure out how she might change things during her time at college. When Manmohan Singh, the first Indian Prime

Minister to do so in a long time, gave his historic speech, she interned in the Congress. In an effort to become a peacemaker, she pursued training in conflict resolution and mediation. She also studied the geopolitical realities of South Asia as a researcher with a Pakistani professor. She remained dissatisfied in spite of all these encounters. She first learned about microfinance in 2005, when she was a senior. Prominent individuals such as Vikram Akula from SKS Microfinance and Pierre Omidyar from the Omidyar Network discussed how millions of women may be empowered by small loans. This idea fascinated her.

Microfinance was not just about giving money—it was about creating financial opportunities that led to real impact. It was a way to bridge the financial gap for women while also building a sustainable business model. For the first time, she realized that solving big global issues like equity, peace, and prosperity required uplifting the masses. And there was no place with more potential for this than India. Even though she had visited India many times as a child, she understood that she knew very little about the real struggles of its people. She decided she needed to learn more. Ajaita had visited India many times while growing up, but she never truly understood the heart of the country— its villages. She believed that to really know India, she had to experience rural life.

From Discovery to Dedication: Choosing Rural India

In 2006, at just 21 years old, she made a bold decision. She would spend a year in India to understand "Bharat," the rural part of the country that shaped the lives of millions. Her parents, living in New York, were shocked. They had expected her to become a lawyer or pursue a more traditional career. But Ajaita felt a strong instinct pushing her in a different direction. To ease their concerns, she told them it was just for a year. In reality, she was determined to follow this path. She joined Ujjivan Financial Services, a small microfinance company at the time. It was India's first urban microfinance institution, and today, it has grown into a massive, publicly listed company. This experience was her first real exposure to how finance could empower people at the grassroots level.

Throughout her time working in the startup, Ajaita gained knowledge beyond her expectations about India alongside its rural complexities and its female population. She became overwhelmed by her affection for India because expressing these feelings proved difficult. She arrived with a blank slate to absorb information about whatever she encountered although she admitted her lack of knowledge. After making the switch to the microfinance industry she spent eight years there instead of the initial gap year she planned to do before law school. She spent time in more than 10,000 villages throughout India while traveling between Karnataka, Andhra Pradesh, Jharkhand, Uttar Pradesh, Bihar, Odisha, Madhya Pradesh, and Chhattisgarh respectively.

Her decision surprised everyone back home, especially her mother. She often joked that she didn't even know how to explain Ajaita's career choices to others. With top academic credentials, Ajaita was expected to become a lawyer, earn a comfortable living in New York, and settle down. Instead, she was navigating some of India's most remote villages, driven by a passion to make a real difference. Ajaita's journey confused many. No one truly understood why Ajaita had chosen this path.

But during those eight years, she discovered something powerful— the resilience of women. She saw their strength, their determination, and their potential. More than just struggling with poverty, rural India was a place of dignity, resourcefulness, and untapped opportunity. With 800 million people living in 700,000 villages, rural India was often overlooked. People lacked access to basic services, and their needs were ignored. But from a business perspective, this was also a massive missed opportunity. Rural India wasn't just a challenge; it was a powerful market waiting to be recognized. Ajaita learned how to bridge this gap. Despite her American accent, she picked up bits of Telugu, Kannada, and fluent Hindi. She learned how to connect with people, understand their needs, and design solutions that truly worked for them.

What kept her going? What was the biggest struggle? She wasn't sure. But one thing was clear—she had found her purpose. Ajaita couldn't ignore the challenges she saw. How could 800 million people live without electricity? How could children die from kerosene fires in their homes? How could farmers, the ones feeding the country and the world, be denied financial services and basic resources? It didn't make sense. This realization became her mission. During her years in microfinance, she launched groundbreaking initiatives—India's first health insurance for urban slum women, the first nationwide life insurance for rural families, and a partnership between Nokia and Airtel to bring mobile phones to the masses. These projects proved one thing: when you see people through a lens of equality and opportunity, everything changes.

For Ajaita, this was thrilling. By 25, she had already driven major social and financial innovations. America no longer excited her—India did. The energy, the potential, and the ability to create real change kept her grounded in rural India.

Building Frontier Markets: An Accidental Entrepreneur

Now, 20 years later, she reflects on that decision with no regrets. But building Frontier Markets was another challenge altogether. It meant going against deeply rooted social norms, stepping into spaces where women were rarely seen as leaders. Yet, she had spent years understanding the pulse of India—the women in remote villages who held immense power within their communities. Ajaita never planned to become an entrepreneur. She calls herself an "accidental entrepreneur" because starting Frontier Markets wasn't the goal—solving a problem was. She saw the massive gap in rural access to essential goods and services. While urban consumers enjoyed the convenience of Amazon and AI-driven recommendations, rural families had no such access. They lacked quality products, reliable services, and the ability to save money on essentials.

Her experience in microfinance had already shown her that women were key to solving this challenge. Women managed households, made daily purchasing decisions, and understood community needs better than anyone. Yet, companies focused only on selling, rarely considering what rural customers actually needed.

Frustrated by ineffective models, Ajaita asked herself: What would actually work?

That's how Frontier Markets was born—a platform designed to bridge this gap by leveraging the power of rural women. Instead of forcing products onto communities, it would listen to them, understand their needs, and empower local women to be the link between businesses and rural customers. But proving that rural women could drive last-mile commerce wasn't easy. She had to fight against deep-seated biases—investors doubted their ability, companies were skeptical, and even communities took time to trust the idea. Yet, she knew that if women were given the right tools and opportunities, they would transform their villages.

And she was right.

Frontier Markets under Ajaita Shah established itself through her dedication to build rural commerce that used women as transformative agents. The vision faced great resistance in persuading people to accept it. At 26 years old, Ajaita pursued her large-scale objective to transform rural distribution while using her American accent to present to investors. Many investors doubted her credibility because she was a young woman without conventional business experience to lead such major transitions. Several investors dismissed the idea completely yet other investors doubted whether rural women could advance supply-chain transformation efforts.

A competition judge showed her great value by suggesting she present her life story before offering her business pitch. It proved to be an essential moment. The business world was unfamiliar to Ajaita because she spent numerous years working with rural women in India instead of coming from traditional business backgrounds.

She shared her trip before talking about her company's approach, using her experience to establish credibility. She adopted Hinglish, a combination of Hindi and English, to communicate with investors and the communities she served, making sure she stayed true to herself while communicating her vision.

Ajaita persevered in the face of criticism, rejection, and distrust. Her perseverance and the eventual success of Frontier Markets were driven by her conviction that empowering women could change entire communities.

Her efforts are changing people's lives. She has demonstrated that tackling issues at the local level may result in significant change by fusing economic and social effects. According to Ajaita, social entrepreneurship is about developing profitable, long-lasting solutions rather than about giving to charities. From an accidental entrepreneur to a global changemaker, her story is one of determination, innovation, and a deep belief in the power of women to reshape the world.

Chapter 17

Anna Wagner Norseng on Ethical Trade in a Man's World

Anna Wagner Norseng is the founder of Anouska AS. The company she established in 2000. It started as a small business importing woven placemats and baskets from Madagascar. However, it has now grown into a thriving enterprise.

Today, Anouska Engros AS operates three retail stores. One is at CC Vest shopping centre in Oslo the other is in Asker, and the third is in Toensberg in Norway. Anna has built a business that stands strong in the competitive retail industry. Her business specializes in a wide variety of goods. The collection includes furniture, mirrors, lamps, glassware, textiles, antiquities, gifts, clothing, and accessories. She works closely with local vendors and craftspeople in China, India, and Indonesia to get most of these items.[59] Anna's entrepreneurial journey is deeply connected to her professional background and extensive international experience. Before starting her business, she spent ten years as a product developer and production manager at Blue Dress/Madam Blue. During this time, she traveled to India nearly 40 times. She gained deep insights into the country's manufacturing industry. These visits helped her build connections and understand the craftsmanship India had to offer. When she started her own business, returning to India as a sourcing hub was a natural choice.

Building a Distinctive Global Supply Chain

From the beginning, Anna knew that success in Norway's competitive market required a unique product range. She had to provide something distinct from the competition. To accomplish this, she frequently attended Delhi's twice-yearly Handicraft Fair. These fairs feature producers from many industries displaying their products. Anna built solid relationships with suppliers and stayed current on industry trends by going. Over time, she expanded her network beyond these trade fairs. Through suggestions or even fortuitous meetings, she frequently discovered new sources. However, she always placed a high premium on exclusivity, thus she purposefully avoided getting her goods from the same factories as her competitors. She says, "Having a distinctive collection is crucial in a small country like Norway." Products manufactured in the same factories as your rivals are not reliable. Years of experience and intuition are the foundation for Anna's product selection approach; she carefully plans her collections and regularly collaborates with manufacturers to develop unique pieces. When a sample is prepared, it is sent to Norway for assessment, and if she believes the product would be popular, she orders it; otherwise, she bypasses the sampling procedure, relying on her gut.

Anna Wagner Norseng's ability to cultivate enduring relationships with her suppliers is key to her success. She has almost a decade of experience dealing with several of the same manufacturers. These collaborations are built on mutual respect, trust, and a commitment to quality. By maintaining a steady supplier base, Anna ensures that her business receives high-quality products while providing stability to the manufacturers.

Anna values cooperation over cost-cutting, in contrast to many companies that regularly switch suppliers to obtain cheaper costs. She knows that a supply chain disruption and quality compromise can result from frequent supplier changes. Instead, she establishes solid alliances founded on honesty and dependability. Anna stays in contact with her suppliers using modern communication tools like email and WhatsApp to guarantee smooth operations and minimize miscommunications. By employing this tactic, she has created a dependable supply chain where both parties benefit from a consistent and productive working relationship. These enduring partnerships have been further reinforced by her dedication to moral and sustainable business practices.

There are several obstacles to overcome when operating an import company. One of the most crucial elements is logistics. Anna has teamed up with a reliable logistics company to guarantee a seamless procedure. For many years, this company has been in charge of shipping commodities from India to Norway. Their background contributes to the process' efficiency and predictability.

The products must pass customs clearance after they reach Norway. They are then brought to Anna's warehouse. She does not have to worry about handling these steps herself. All payments and financial records are handled by a committed bookkeeper. This guarantees timely reconciliations and correct transactions. With these dependable processes in place, Anna can concentrate on expanding her company. She doesn't need to become tied down in paperwork. She can instead focus on choosing products, building relationships with suppliers, and growing her clientele. Her success has been primarily attributed to her methodical approach.

For Anna, quality control comes first. She goes out of her way to ensure her items are up to par. Although she rarely receives customer complaints, she resolves any problems promptly and effectively. Most issues are resolved by offering discounts or credit notes. To correct errors, some vendors would instead recreate the products. Strong connections with suppliers and consumers are maintained due to this dedication to quality.

Conducting business between Norway and India is not always simple. Bureaucratic obstacles can slow down operations. However, the process is made easier by the fact that many of the goods Anna purchases are duty-free.

Prioritizing Ethics, Quality, and Sustainability

Anna is strongly committed to producing ethically. She thinks that ethical behaviour and corporate success should go hand in hand. To guarantee this, she only collaborates with factories that adhere to stringent labour and safety regulations. Twice a year, she personally inspects the working conditions of her suppliers. Thanks to this practical approach, she can confirm that workers are treated properly and enjoy a safe workplace. Choosing the correct suppliers is only one aspect of her dedication to ethical sourcing. Because of her enduring ties, she has been able to promote constructive change in the supply chain throughout the years. She has persuaded manufacturers to embrace more sustainable methods and better labor practices by preserving good connections with them.

Anna is aware that moral business conduct is advantageous to all parties. Employees receive just compensation and secure employment, and companies establish a reputation for honesty and excellence. She is adamant that businesses ought to accomplish more than just turn a profit. They ought to support ethical production and fair trade as ways to benefit society. Her commitment to these principles has aided in developing a reputable and trustworthy brand. Anna's experience working in diverse cultures has given her important insights into how people think and behave in the workplace. She now values her Indian companions' friendliness and warmth. Since these characteristics are not as strongly valued in Norwegian society, she finds their strong work ethic and profound reverence for elders particularly noteworthy.

Navigating Cultural Differences and Gender Barriers

However, there are drawbacks to conducting business in India as well. The way she solves problems is one significant difference she has noticed. In Norway, issues are usually dealt with head-on, emphasizing finding prompt and practical solutions. People prefer open discussions and immediate resolutions. On the other hand, Anna has seen that when issues emerge, some of her Indian suppliers seek to sidestep direct conflict. Sometimes, they wait for direction or expect that problems will work themselves out before taking action.

This cultural difference has required Anna to adjust her expectations and approach. She has improved her ability to speak effectively, be patient, and offer comfort when required. Over time, she has devised ways to reconcile these disparities, guaranteeing more seamless company operations while preserving solid ties with her suppliers.

Anna has encountered gender-based challenges as a woman in a male-dominated industry, especially in India. Traditional views on women still influence business interactions. She avoids using public transit, dresses modestly and avoids going out alone at night in order to protect herself. These actions draw attention to the wider gender inequalities in Indian society, even though they are required.

Anna has taken the initiative to teach her suppliers about gender equality in an attempt to remedy this problem. She stresses that harassment is not tolerated, and that men and women are treated equally in Norway. Despite these challenges, she remains committed to fostering respect and understanding between cultures. Anna values cultural exchange and enjoys sharing Norwegian customs with her Indian partners. Many of them have travelled to Norway to see her, even staying at her house as guests. These trips foster mutual understanding of diverse cultures and improve commercial ties.

She has seen major changes in India during the last 35 years. The nation has changed due to the proliferation of mobile phones and internet access, which has increased awareness and connectedness. She has seen, meanwhile, that growing living expenses are having an effect on the purchasing power of companies such as hers. Despite these changes, traditional crafts continue to play a significant role in her firm. Indian craftspeople ensure the ongoing need for handcrafted goods by passing down their knowledge from generation to generation. She does point out, though, that younger generations are becoming more interested in new jobs, which may provide problems for traditional craftsmen in the future.

Advice for Future Entrepreneurs

Reflecting on her experience, Anna offers valuable insights for anyone wishing to launch a company in India. She stresses the importance of preparing ahead, being organized, and working hard. Production and shipment might take several months, so managing an import business demands patience. Businesses need sufficient money to manage cash flow and maintain seamless operations. In Norway, clients may take up to 30 days to pay, while many firms want upfront payments before beginning production.

Anna also highlights the importance of market research. A product that enjoys popularity in India fails to predict market success in Norway. To succeed, entrepreneurs must examine the pricing habits and patterns and customer preferences within their target market. Knowledge of how consumers behave enables businesses to make improved decisions for their operations. She advises newer business owners to build reliable relationships between logistics companies and suppliers. The regions demand firms that excel in dependability and trust. A trader needs to persevere while demonstrating flexibility and strategic thinking to succeed in international markets. The success of Anna's story proves that companies reaching international markets through proper strategy successfully connect different markets and cultures while retaining sustainable quality standards.

Tenacity, flexibility, and moral leadership have shaped the path of Anna Wagner Norseng. She has achieved business success through her focus on quality and the development of long-term client relationships and cultural understanding. Her dedication to overcoming field challenges through principled action makes her emerge as an outstanding leader. Successful businesspeople can find their road to success by studying the example of Anna through her ongoing tale of integrity alongside determination and commitment. She established a thriving business that supports moral commerce between Norway and India through her persistent learning practices and strong commitment to values.

Chapter 18

Vidya Basarkod on Navigating Indian and Nordic Leadership

Vidya Basarkod has been the India Managing Director for Ramboll and the Director of Ramboll's Engineering Center in Delhi. She has spent more than 40 years in civil and structural engineering, heading teams working both for India and worldwide, specifically Scandinavia and has charted the path for change in what is still largely a male-dominated industry.

In this chapter, we delve into the distinction between Indian and Nordic leadership, the challenges of being the lone woman in the room, and how businesses can build more diverse workplaces. Vidya, having led both in India and a Danish corporation, points out notable contrasts between the Scandinavian and Indian styles of leadership. Leadership is developing with new stories, ambiguity, and DEI issues. The Scandinavian style has a strong base with planning, data-driven and consensus-driven approaches. A principal area for strengthening is making flexibility more adaptive for dealing with issues of implementation.

Nordic leaders prioritize planning, analysis of data, and building consensus. Decisions are made after exhaustive discussions to ensure that all stakeholders are heard. This approach creates inclusivity and well-informed decisions. Nevertheless, she explains that flexibility when implementing can be a problem at times. Decision-making in Nordic leadership is systematic, but real-world implementation sometimes demands flexibility with changing variables.

Conversely, Indian leadership is practical in execution and amenable to rapid adjustments in unforeseen circumstances. In India's fast-paced business landscape, leaders expect problems, modify strategies, and move ahead with implementation. Nevertheless, Vidya feels that Indian leaders can learn from more emphasis on planning and evidence-based decision-making, like the Norwegians. She points out that both leadership models have positives and areas of development and have a lot to learn from each.

Vidya is a post-graduate structural engineer from IIT Mumbai and specializes in Infrastructure Development, especially in Airports and Metro Rail sectors. She led the planning and designing of Mumbai Metro Line 1 and provided consultancy services to major corporations such as Zurich Airport and GMR. Her career objective has centred on constructing physical structures to build the nation.

She shares her professional journey at Ramboll Infrastructure, an Engineering and Architecture consultancy firm based in Copenhagen, Denmark. Ramboll has operated in India for almost 3 decades now and has accomplished a mutual exchange of expertise by benefiting from Indian engineering expertise. Vidya considers her tenure in Ramboll as one of the most rewarding phases in her professional journey since the company supported sustainability and inclusive leadership. Working for Ramboll has been among her best professional experiences, fitting ideally with her values while serving as Managing Director and GCC Director for nine years.

As for being the only woman in the room, she seldom felt that way. She emphasized preparation, performance, and ongoing improvement over gender. Women leaders must own their strengths—resilience, flexibility, empathy, and authenticity—without attempting to fit into a mould. She wants women to adopt these as virtues, not try to become stereotypical leaders, because authenticity makes leaders more impactful. This mindset promotes leadership, turning diversity into a strength instead of a weakness. But with more and more discussion about gender diversity, she admits that women leaders have strengths that differ from those of men. These put them in a better situation as leaders, especially in the current business environment where abounding uncertainties call for such leadership traits.

Engineering, particularly civil and structural engineering, continues to be dominated by men globally. The high-stress aspect of on-site work, remote project sites, and physical demands have dissuaded women from pursuing careers in these fields in the past. Industry culture is, however, evolving with the understanding that a diverse labour force is required to provide infrastructure for the future.

Tech areas such as computer science and IT have traditionally been more appealing to women, but with automation and AI filling the job market, interest in fundamental engineering fields is increasing. Vidya feels that employment security in conventional engineering is now higher than in fast-changing tech fields. She recognizes that the sector did not create a compelling story for women in civil engineering. The absence of role models, secure work environments, and career guidance contributed to the disparity. Companies are now taking positive steps to create more diverse workplaces by encouraging women into executive positions and providing safer, more accommodating work environments.

The largest gender difference remains in engineering jobs on construction sites, where females are reluctant to enter project manager and construction manager jobs. Whereas women are abundantly represented within planning and designing, leadership on-site is an area of difficulty. Vidya remains hopeful that further efforts will lead to a dwindling of the gap.

India and the Nordic countries

One of the greatest strengths of Nordic leadership, Vidya maintains, is a focus on sustainability and social influence. In India, sustainability has been more of an ancillary business priority, but it is central to the strategy in Nordic firms. Ramboll's business motto, "Partners for Sustainable Change," is illustrative of that focus. Vidya says Indian firms might learn from weaving sustainability into business models instead of viewing it as an add-on.

Conversely, she urges Nordic leaders to pay more attention to India, given its strategic importance, skilled workforce, and rapidly growing economy. Understanding and navigating India's complex business environment can create valuable opportunities for Nordic companies. Vidya has also been a proponent of gender diversity initiatives in the engineering and technical sectors. Part of the solution is to get deserving current women leaders promoted to leadership positions. The prominence of powerful female role models encourages young women to eliminate self-doubt and realize actual career prospects in the field. At Ramboll, this model has worked effectively, and a robust female leadership team has resulted. Ramboll has also transitioned from a cost-arbitrage to a value-arbitrage model, i.e., Indian engineers are no longer merely doing work but are involved in intricate planning and designs and sustainability-oriented projects. This has also made jobs in engineering more appealing to women.

Challenges of Women

While cultural differences exist, Vidya believes that women leaders worldwide share common challenges. Whether in India or the Nordics, women juggle dual responsibilities of career and family, and male-dominated industries often create barriers to advancement. Through interactions with Nordic women leaders, she has noted parallel issues in work-life balance, gender prejudice, and representation of leadership. She comforts young professionals by telling them that these challenges are not country-specific but universal, demanding systemic transformation.

Updating the Industrial Trend

In encouraging young women to aim for STEM leadership roles, Vidya stresses the following:

It is essential to remain current on Industry Trends. Monitoring global trends, best practices, and technological innovations keeps one relevant in a fast-changing industry.

Upskilling Continuously – In addition to technical competencies, leaders need to comprehend business dynamics, such as the commercial, environmental, and economic implications of their activities. Another method is establishing strong networks through interactions with industry colleagues, both men and women. This promotes knowledge sharing and career development.

Authenticity in Leadership is equally important. Women must harness their strengths, including empathy, flexibility, and resilience, and there is no need to follow the stereotypical leadership pattern of men. Vidya finds authenticity to be the mantra of success in global workplaces. Indian professionals are inclined by nature to be culturally sensitive, thanks to India's multicultural setup. Vidya offers the following tips for women:

Remain authentic in values and strengths when working in multicultural teams.

Establish deep and honest working relationships because effective collaboration can only thrive among strong relationships.

Celebrate differences instead of forcing oneself into some kind of predefined mould.

As we close this chapter, Vidya's journey through leadership, engineering, and gender inclusivity provides sound advice for professionals in both the Indian and Nordic worlds. Her experience is a tribute to shattering barriers, honest leadership, and making real workplace changes. Her advice to young women in STEM is straightforward: Be informed, be confident, own your strengths, and proactively pursue leadership positions. With shifting industry attitudes and increasing gender inclusivity initiatives, the future is bright for women in engineering and leadership across the globe.

Part 4

Chapter 19

Men as Allies - Supporting Women

In this section, we explore the crucial role men play as allies in advancing gender equality. From partners and fathers to business leaders and policymakers, male allies have a profound impact on breaking down barriers and fostering inclusive leadership.

A powerful example of this is Masud Gharahkhani, President of the Storting and Norway's second-highest-ranking official after the Prime Minister. Gharahkhani has made equality, democracy, and the fight against injustice central to his mission. His advocacy is deeply personal, shaped by his upbringing and the influence of strong women in his life, particularly his mother, whose perseverance and ambition shaped his understanding of gender equality.

Gharahkhani emphasizes that Norway's success is not just built on oil but on human capital—where gender equality plays a fundamental role. Yet, despite Norway's progressive policies, women remain underrepresented in the private sector. He believes that true diversity strengthens organizations and that awareness must continue to grow to ensure equal representation across industries.

This section highlights how men—including husbands, fathers, business leaders, and entrepreneurs—can actively support women in achieving leadership positions. Through personal stories, reflections, and concrete actions, Part 4 explores the role of male allies in shaping a more inclusive and equitable future.

Chapter 20
Christian Ringnes on Championing Women

Credit: Ole Walter Jacobsen

One of the most well-known businesspeople and benefactors in Norway is Christian Ringnes. His contributions to Oslo's artistic and cultural landscape have earned him recognition. He is a self-made businessman who has been instrumental in using sculpture and art to change public areas. One of his most famous projects is the Ekeberg Sculpture Park.

Christian is a strong advocate for gender parity and social equality in addition to his work in Norway. He opposes established conventions and backs programs that encourage diversity. Christian is also involved in global artistic collaborations. He supports 'Artdom', an initiative that connects Indian and British artists. This initiative promotes the creation of collaborative works by artists from various backgrounds. They transcend cultural gaps and have meaningful conversations via art. Numerous renowned Indian painters have participated in this project.

British artists have collaborated with artists like as Raja Ravi Sharma, Anita Dey, and Meera Nambiar to create distinctive and impactful works. Christian's conviction that art can bring people together across boundaries is reflected in this effort. Christian Ringnes continues to have a significant influence through his activism, generosity, and support of international art. His work is motivated by a strong desire to improve the future and give back.

Christian's views on Gender Equality

He expresses his opinions on gender equality and participates in in-depth discussions regarding men helping women. His arguments are clear and well-defined. According to him, equality means giving everyone the same chances in life and at work. He does, however, stress that equal chances alone are insufficient for actual gender equality. He is adamant that establishing equilibrium in fields where males have historically held a dominant position requires proactive measures. He adds, "We also need to assist in creating more balance than there has traditionally been." Christian emphasizes how crucial awareness is to see and ending discriminating behaviour. He talks about his upbringing in response to a question on why he supports gender equality. He witnessed directly the restrictions imposed on women, even in his own home, having grown up with two strong sisters and a dedicated mother.

He recalls, "Especially my eldest sister, she was encouraged to do a secretary education instead of something where she could end up as a boss. I always found that quite strange and unfair." This early exposure to gender biases shaped his strong commitment to advocating for change. As Christian gained professional experience and joined board positions, his awareness of gender inequality grew. He began questioning the issue more deeply.

Questions Raised

Why women? Who makes the majority of customer decisions? Are they underrepresented in business leadership? Why, when we know that 70 to 80% of all consumption is decided by women, do they not have more decision-making power in business?

These observations strengthened his determination to accelerate progress. He strongly believes that systematic change is necessary to achieve true equality. He states, "If it was only a club for men doing fly fishing, beards, and shooting, I think it's fine. But this club has influential members, and with influence comes responsibility."

This demonstrates his conviction that those in positions of authority must advance equitable representation and build a more harmonious society. By questioning the established order of the Norske Selskab, Norway's most elite men's club, Christian made a daring move. This turned into one of his most well-known campaigns for gender equality.

Despite significant resistance from members who insisted the club should remain male-only, he remained vocal about inclusivity. He argued that exclusivity in influential spaces limited progress and fairness.

Interestingly, some women also opposed the change. They preferred their husbands to remain in male-only environments. This, Christian observed, reflected deep-rooted cultural complexities in gender issues.

He firmly thinks that people should be valued for their contributions to society rather than their wealth. His advocacy for change was not limited to exclusive clubs. He believed that privilege comes with responsibility. His perspective on life and leadership have been shaped by his grandmother's guidance, which he often recalls when reflecting on his ideas. This idea drives his efforts to create opportunities for others to succeed, especially women. Christian talks about his attempts to instil in his children the values of independence and responsibility. He acknowledges the challenges of parenting children in affluent surroundings while highlighting the need of setting a good example. According to him, actions speak louder than words, "Children will see what you do, and that is what they're going to learn." This highlights how important it is to set an example instead of just giving directions.

Christian also considers the societal shifts he has seen throughout time. He points out that women are becoming more and more dominant in Norway's public sector and higher education. He forecasts a change in gender dynamics in the ensuing decades based on this trend. "We have a quota system today where at least 40% must be women, but in 20 years, it might be men who need the quota," he speculates. He is concerned that young men are falling behind women in a variety of sectors despite these developments. He stresses the importance of providing both sexes with equal support. Christian also discusses privilege and its connection to responsibility. He was brought up with a strong sense of duty to contribute to society. One of his grandmother's quotes is, "A person's worth is determined by how much they contribute to society." He has lived his entire life following this idea. "My mother used to remind us that fairness isn't about giving everyone the same but about making sure everyone gets what they need to succeed," he says, sharing a heartwarming story from his early years. "That stuck with me."

Christian also discusses generational shifts and the role of younger men in advancing gender equality. He expresses optimism about how new generations embrace fairness and inclusion more naturally.

He states, "I see a lot of young men who are actively supporting their women colleagues and partners. It gives me hope." However, he cautions against complacency as well. He stresses that advancement necessitates constant work and shouldn't be taken for granted. "Equality cannot be taken for granted. We have to work on it every day," he emphasizes.

Christian reminds men that it's acceptable not to know everything and promotes an open-minded attitude to gender activism. The ability to listen, learn, and develop is what counts most. "It's acceptable to not know everything," he shares. Your willingness to listen and learn is what matters. His observations are incredibly intimate, moulded by times of introspection and personal development. He freely confesses his prior transgressions and how they have shaped his life. Rather than deterring others, he encourages and motivates men to approach gender advocacy with humility and an open mind. He believes that real change comes from continuous learning and self-awareness.

Christian Ringnes considers how his background and life experiences have influenced his idea of giving back to society. While he always carried his grandmother's words about the value of giving back, he emphasizes that before one can give on a large scale, one must first have something to give. Despite growing up in a well-to-do family, Christian did not inherit wealth early. He explains, "It wasn't abundant, and I certainly didn't touch any of my heritage until much later in life. So, in many ways, I consider myself self-made." He reflects on how, during the early stages of building his business, his ability to give was limited. However, as his success grew, so did his capacity to contribute meaningfully. He notes, "It's not only about the desire to give – it's also about the ability to do so."

His approach to philanthropy developed gradually rather than through a single defining moment. He describes it as a series of experiences and projects that sparked his interest. He draws inspiration from the Indian concept of 'duco favors'—a system of mutual support where people help each other and, in turn, give back to the world. This idea, he explains, was always present in him but became more actionable as the right opportunities appeared. Christian found his gateway to philanthropy through art and sculptures. He shares, "It started in Oslo, first through my company, which I didn't fully own at the time, and then later through personal giving." Over time, he became more focused on projects that genuinely interested him. He believes that while many people donate to various causes, true commitment comes when a cause aligns with personal passion. He observes that people often take years to find a cause that truly resonates with them. "It might be the Ukraine war, animal welfare, or something else, but over five or ten years, people stumble upon something that touches their heart, and then they become committed supporters."

Dynamics of wealth and privilege

Christian also considers the broader dynamics of wealth and privilege. He acknowledges that the way wealth is distributed globally affects how people think about giving. However, he believes that regardless of the financial scale, the principle of giving remains the same giving back because the world has provided opportunities.

When advising others on contributing to a cause, Christian emphasizes the importance of awareness. He states, "First and foremost, it's about recognizing the biases and challenges around us. There's a lot of gender discrimination that exists simply because people don't think about it." He admits that he, too, was shaped by the beliefs of his generation. "For instance, the notion that a woman stays at home while the man works was a given in my parents' time, but the world has changed tremendously."

Once awareness is achieved, Christian believes the possibilities for action are immense. He suggests that people can provide opportunities, advocate publicly, and help women progress. However, he acknowledges that change takes time. "Progress occurs, but its outcome or impact becomes clear only after a certain period." He cites Norway as an example, where women now make up more than half of university graduates and dominate fields like public administration and politics. Christian also reflects on the shifting global attitudes toward gender preferences and roles. He notes that cultural perspectives continue to evolve. "It used to be that families preferred having sons, but now there's growing recognition of the value women bring—not just as individuals but as contributors to society." He believes this shift is a sign of progress and wisdom. "Women tend to be more giving and empathetic, qualities that are invaluable."

Christian Ringnes asserts that leaving a legacy means passing on opportunities and values to the next generation in addition to acquiring material wealth. "Giving back is about setting an example, not about ego or recognition," he says. Through advocacy, words, or deeds, you can motivate others, and you have completed a significant duty.

While he remains optimistic about gender equality, he acknowledges the challenges that come with progress. "We're moving toward what could be an almost perfect balance between genders. But with this shift, we might face another problem – young men falling out of the system." He observes that women are excelling in many fields, sometimes outcompeting men. This shift, while positive, creates new challenges that society must address.

When considering his larger giving-back philosophy, Ringnes connects his views on generosity and equality with the concept of legacy. His life story demonstrates the strength of deliberate action, from his early teachings on charity to his support of public art and fight for gender equality. He believes that true impact is not just about donating resources but also about creating opportunities for others and challenging traditional norms that hold people back.

Looking ahead, Christian remains hopeful. Although he admits that sometimes progress seems gradual, he is confident in the long-term improvement. "The world goes in trends, and even though we might not always see results right away, we are on the correct track. We can create a more just world for coming generations as long as we remain dedicated, keep pointing out prejudices, and back projects that align with our principles." He has demonstrated, via his support of gender equality and inclusivity, that they are not solely women's concerns but rather are shared obligations. "Everyone gains when society promotes equality."

As the discussion comes to an end, Christian considers the wider effects of gender equality. In his ideal world, desire, talent, and abilities—rather than gender—determine success. According to him, levelling the playing field is necessary to guarantee that everyone has an equal chance to achieve. He encourages listeners to make little but meaningful changes in their own lives, such as overcoming bias, coaching a colleague, or being conscious of their choices. "Every little step counts," he says in closing. We can change things together.

Chapter 21

Sindre Finnes, Parul Soni, and Christian Lund: Men Who Move Mountains

0This chapter tells the stories of Sindre, Christian, and Parul—three men who support gender equality in their own ways. Their experiences demonstrate how collaborations and forward-thinking ideas may overcome assumptions. They demonstrate that men can contribute significantly to the creation of a future in which success is not determined by a person's gender by questioning conventions and advocating for equal opportunities.

Women are their own greatest champions in the fight for equality. However, many men also stand beside them in this journey. This chapter celebrates three extraordinary men who actively support their wives and advocate for gender balance. They are Sindre Finnes, Christian Lund and Parul Soni. Their stories show how partnership, persistence, and a progressive mindset can create a more inclusive society.

Sindre Finnes: Redefining the Role of the "First Man"

Sindre Finnes is an economist and a leader in the Norwegian industry. He is well-recognized as the spouse of former Norwegian Prime Minister Erna Solberg (2013–2022). Sindre accepted his position as "the first man" under Erna. He said it was a fun and rewarding experience. He had great advantages but no direct political obligations, unlike his wife. "It's a lot of fun," Sindre said. "You can go to concerts, join official delegations, and meet people from all over the world—without doing the big work."

Though his position was unique, he noticed that the club of men in similar roles is growing. Husbands of women leaders—such as Angela Merkel's husband—are now forming a network of support.

"It's starting to expand," he added. "There are now four female prime ministers."

Parul Soni: Identifying International Role Models

In India, Parul Soni is a fervent supporter of gender equality and sustainability. He thinks Sindre's approach is admirable and a good example. "It's wonderful to see men supporting women's leadership and development," Parul said. He compared the situation in India and Norway and stressed the need for global role models. Regarding gender equality, he declared, "Norway and the Nordic countries are amazing. However, the numbers could use improvement even there. We need more leaders like Sindre to push for change."

Christian Lund: Supporting a Powerful Woman

Kristin Skogen Lund, the CEO of Schibsted and one of the most powerful women in Norway, is married to Christian Lund. He offered insights into her leadership and accomplishments. Kristin's success stems from her commitment, skill, and diligence. But Christian believes her people skills set her apart. He remarked, "She has incredible empathy, fairness, and interactive skills. She speaks up when necessary, but she also lets others shine." Although Kristin dislikes conflict, she does not avoid it either. "She handles conflicts immediately," Christian explained. "And even when speaking out against influential people, she doesn't hesitate to do so." She inspires and persuades others with her powerful communication abilities. Christian considers her one of the best communicators he has ever seen.

A Strong Support System

Christian underlined how crucial Kristin's achievement was to her family, mentors, and a nurturing environment. At home, he also makes sure that everyone shares chores. "After I met her, I tried to support her at every step," he said. "I take my share of the daily logistics and challenges."

Kristin's ability to handle powerful people and difficult conversations is rare among women, according to studies. Christian believes these are qualities future women leaders can learn from.

The Power of Partnership

These three men—Sindre, Parul, and Christian—show that gender equality is a shared responsibility. They prove that when men support women, society benefits as a whole. Their experiences demonstrate the value of teamwork. They contribute to the development of a society in which aptitude, not gender, determines success by dispelling stereotypes, distributing duties, and supporting women in leadership roles.

India faces significant gender inequality in economic participation. In the World Economic Forum's 2021 Global Gender Gap Report, India came in at number 140 out of 156 nations. Parul Soni, Founder & Secretary General, Association of Business Women in Commerce and Industry (ABWCI), works to overcome barriers that keep women from moving up the business ladder. Addressing the systemic obstacles that keep women from becoming successful business owners is his aim.

Creating a Support System for Women Entrepreneurs

Parul noticed that fewer women were starting businesses compared to men. He wanted to understand why and find solutions. "Not many women were coming forward," Parul explained. "The reasons were challenges like lack of access to finance, lack of appropriate market linkages, supportive ecosystems, and under-utilization of technology solutions for better efficiency."

He created ABWCI, a global Chamber of Commerce for women businesses, to address this. This platform offers technology, training, and business possibilities to support the development and success of female entrepreneurs.

According to Parul, women require a single location where they can obtain - Financial support, Networking opportunities, and Business training. His approach attempts to give women sustainable possibilities and reduce the gender gap in economic participation. Christian Lund admitted that women are less inclined than men to take chances in their business ventures, even in Norway.

Despite Norway's commitment to gender equality, societal and cultural hurdles still affect women in the workplace. Christian emphasized that further support is necessary to inspire more women to consider business. Male colleagues resisted him, asking why he was concentrating on women's empowerment. Some women's organizations were also wary of having a guy in charge of their cause at the time. They were concerned that a male voice would take over their area. Despite these challenges, Parul remained committed. He engaged with the government, business leaders, and civil society to promote women's economic empowerment. His story challenges long-standing social norms and serves as a reminder of the value of understanding, tolerance, and tenacity.

Progress in Equality

A larger initiative to reduce the gender gap in business includes Parul's work in India. His initiatives demonstrate that continued support, understanding, and action are necessary for gender equality, as do viewpoints from around the world like Christians'.

In difficult positions, Sindre Finnes emphasized how technology has benefited both men and women. Workplaces are now more flexible, thanks to advanced technology, which makes it easier for people to manage their personal and professional lives. Women have benefited greatly from this flexibility. It has made it possible for them to balance their family obligations with professional success. Sindre observed, "Technology has made it easier to work efficiently and do a good job." "Women have taken advantage of that."

Leadership and Gender: A Shared Approach

When discussing leadership styles, Sindre and Christian agreed that leadership is not gender specific. They have observed that in Norwegian politics, both male and female leaders share similar qualities, values, and goals.

Sindre says, "In politics, I don't see a major difference in how men and women lead."

Christian believes that this also applies to the corporate world. Christian says, "Kristin sees herself as a leader." She does not consider herself a "woman leader and gender doesn't really matter to her. That said, traits like empathy and interpersonal skills may be more common in women leaders, but it's hard to generalize."

Empowering Women Leaders in India and Globally

Parul shared his vision for a more inclusive business ecosystem with more women leaders in India and globally.

"That's my mission," he said. "We need leadership at every level—village, district, state, and national. Economic and political leadership must go hand in hand." He highlighted his initiative to support women village heads, believing this is where change must begin. "Village-level leadership is often overlooked. These women have immense potential, but they remain invisible. My goal is to create interventions that help them step into leadership roles."

Despite the current underrepresentation of women in leadership, Parul is optimistic. "In the coming years, we'll see more women emerging as political and economic leaders. Change is happening, and it's gaining momentum. However, economic empowerment should be the driving force. Social change takes time, but financial independence can bring immediate results."

Parental Leave and Changing Norms

Christian shared his personal experience of taking parental leave in the 1990s. At that time, it was uncommon for men to take time off for childcare.

Christian reflected

"Twenty-five years ago, it was very unusual for a man to take parental leave," he recalled. "In less than three years, we had four children—two pairs of twins. It was too much. Kristin was establishing her profession at the time, and I was a partner at a large legal firm. We came to the conclusion that this couldn't be sustained. However, I never thought Kristin should back off simply because she was the mother.

I took six months of parental leave. It was unusual for guys to do so at the time. Fathers sharing equal responsibility is far more typical these days. For women to advance in their jobs without feeling conflicted between work and family, this change has been essential." He added.

Christian made the decision to move to a more flexible work after weighing their options, despite the fact that doing so would result in a 90% pay reduction. He said, "It was the natural thing to do." "I was able to take on more tasks at home because my new employment afforded me more freedom. I've never regretted my choice to support Kristin's career. In addition to having a fantastic career in another industry, I have, above all, spent a lot more time with my kids than I would have if I had remained at the legal firm."

Christian views work-life balance as more than just one person—male or female—staying at home all day.

"It's about finding roles that allow for balance. Among my friends, I see more men making similar choices. While some social environments still hold on to old norms, the overall trend is moving in the right direction."

Since the 1990s, Norway has evolved. As a result of changing work-life balance and gender roles, more men are increasingly taking parental leave. The government promotes active parenting on the part of both fathers and mothers. He further explained, "Norway has policies that encourage both parents to be involved." Because of this, women can now pursue jobs without feeling compelled to choose between work and family.

Parul Soni saw that parental responsibilities were changing in India, particularly among the middle class. A more balanced approach is being taken by younger generations, in which both men and women actively participate in child rearing. However, there are still structural issues. The absence of institutional childcare is a significant problem that hinders women's ability to pursue employment. "Younger generations are starting to embrace shared parenting. While India doesn't have institutional childcare like the Nordics, more men are stepping up at home. However, this shift is mostly seen in cities and educated communities."

Parental leave and gender equality are two examples of Norway's progressive legislation that have been essential in enabling both parents to participate actively in their children's upbringing. Christian Lund and Kristin Skogen Lund had to make significant changes in order to balance their work and family lives.

Four Key Barriers for Women in Business

The early 2000s marked the beginning of Parul's march toward gender equality. He saw a dearth of women taking the initiative to launch their own companies. After further research, his team identified four key challenges holding women back:

Access to finance – Many women struggle to get loans without a male guarantor.

Access to markets – Women face challenges in reaching the right customers.

Entrepreneurial ecosystems – Business networks and mentorship programs often exclude women.

Access to technology – Many women lack the digital tools and training needed for business growth.

Although these issues are present everywhere, social institutions in India make them worse. As an illustration of pervasive gender bias, many banks require women to have a male guarantor when they apply for loans.

Building a Support System

Parul believed that an organized strategy was required to address these obstacles. He had an idea in 2009 for an ecosystem that would enable women to create profitable small enterprises. The establishment of the first-ever Global Chamber of Commerce for business women was one of the major accomplishments. Women from all around the world may interact, learn, and develop on this platform. It offers them business opportunities, tenders, knowledge-sharing webinars and other courses.

Integrating a virtual model with the Chamber facilitates women's engagement in business-to-business and business-to-consumer interactions. The objective is to provide a one-stop shop where women can get networking opportunities, financial guidance, and technical support to expand their enterprises.

"This journey has been deeply rewarding. Seeing the progress we've made fills me with pride.", says Parul. Leaders like Sindre Finnes and Christian Lund inspire him, and he believes that the model can serve as a blueprint for developing countries like India and others worldwide. The growing global interest in our work is proof of its impact.

Christian shared his perspective

"It's amazing to hear that. Women take fewer risks than males, even in Norway, where gender equality is widely regarded. They are, therefore underrepresented in startups and entrepreneurship. We still need to do more to support and encourage them."

Challenging Social Norms in India

The conversation then shifted to social norms in India. Parul Soni reflected on his experience as a man advocating for gender equality in a patriarchal society. "I began advocating for women's economic empowerment around 13 or 14 years ago," he said. However, I quickly saw that empowerment needed to be connected to economic growth in order to be effective. Jobs in the corporate or public sectors weren't sufficient. True development required wealth creation through entrepreneurship."

However, Parul faced resistance from both men and women. Male colleagues questioned why he was focusing on women's issues. Women's organizations worried he might overshadow their efforts. Despite this, he remained patient and persistent. "I listened to their concerns and worked to build a coalition of stakeholders—including businesses, government, and civil society."

Overcoming Policy Challenges

Another challenge Parul highlighted was how women's issues were often grouped with other categories, such as disabilities. This diluted the focus on gender equality. "We must exert great effort to convince stakeholders of the value of women's economic participation."

Sindre Finnes discussed observations from Norway, highlighting the role that technology has had in fostering a more harmonious workplace. "In Norway, everyone, particularly women, now finds it simpler to balance hard employment with personal obligations because of the widespread availability of technology, including PCs, smartphones, and remote work tools. Technology has revolutionized working from home, in a cabin, or on public transit. Women, in particular, have leveraged this to advance professionally," he noted.

Norway's Gender Quota–A Double-Edged Sword

Norway's 40% gender quota for boards of listed companies and public enterprises has been an interesting case study.

Sindre reflected on its impact

"The quota ensured diversity, but it also had a downside. Many talented women were recruited into board roles rather than executive positions. As a result, fewer women became CEOs of their own companies. However, over time, as more women gained boardroom experience, we saw them move into top leadership roles—leading major companies like DNB and Schibsted. Now, the quota is less necessary because women are naturally stepping into these roles."

Christian agreed but emphasized the need to build leadership at all levels.

"The quota achieved its goal—it increased diversity and inspired other countries to consider similar measures. But now, we must focus on developing women leaders in mid-management and executive roles. Quotas should serve as a reminder, not a crutch." Parul believes that India can learn from Norway. While quotas can be effective, they must be part of a broader system that supports women at all leadership levels. He emphasizes that economic empowerment should be the catalyst for social change.

Why Are There Still More Men at the Top?

A key question being asked is; Why do men still dominate top leadership positions?

Sindre acknowledged that some gender gaps will remain. "Certain responsibilities at home may always be more associated with men or women. However, younger generations are much better at sharing responsibilities than our generation was."

Parul offered a hopeful perspective, highlighting India's progress in the past two decades. "We've made significant strides—improving nutrition, reducing female infanticide, and increasing education for girls. For the first time, India has recorded more girls being born than boys. If we continue pushing for equal opportunities, we won't just close the gender gap—we will surpass expectations."

Christian provided a nuanced view, drawing from his experience in law. "Some fields remain male-dominated. In Norway, 70% of law students are women, yet most senior law firm leaders are men. Women often make different career choices, prioritizing work-life balance over climbing to the top. While personal choices play a role, that doesn't mean we shouldn't work to create more opportunities and stronger support systems."

Cultural norms also influence gender roles. Christian shared an experience from his visits to India: "Every time I go, people ask, 'Where is your wife?' When I explain that she's working while I'm with the kids, they look astonished. I hope these conversations encourage people to rethink traditional roles."

The discussion then turned to education as a key driver of gender equality. Parul emphasized the gap between urban and rural areas: "India is a land of contrasts. While cities are advancing rapidly, rural areas—where most of the population lives—are still behind. Education is the bridge to equality. It shapes mindsets and empowers women to take control of their futures."

Sindre added that real change goes beyond policies—it requires a shift in perception:

"Seeing women succeed in leadership roles inspires others. But we also need men to step up, share responsibilities, and actively support women in overcoming barriers." As the conversation came to a close, Sindre offered a thoughtful perspective: "Some aspects of the gap may never fully close, and that's okay. Men and women bring different strengths to the table, and that diversity can be a good thing. What matters most is building a world where those differences are equally valued."

Parul expressed optimism but emphasized the need for continued effort: "We are moving in the right direction, but we must keep pushing forward. This year's International Women's Day theme, 'Gender Equality for a Stable Future,' reminds us of our shared responsibility. India and South Asia have the potential to lead this movement, but it will require a collective effort."

Christian reflected on the progress made: "Some gaps will close completely, while others may persist due to personal choices and priorities. What matters is that we see incremental change. Every step forward gives me hope. It's a journey, and every effort counts." The discussion highlighted the power of collaboration and shared responsibility. Whether through economic empowerment, education, or cultural shifts, the message was clear: progress is possible, but it demands sustained effort from everyone.

Part 5

Chapter 22

India's It Gender Balance - A Model For The Nordics

India has emerged as an unexpected leader in female representation in the tech industry. Women make up nearly 35% of the IT workforce in India, a figure higher than in many Western countries, including the Nordics. Meanwhile, despite being global pioneers in gender equality, the Nordic countries struggle with female participation in IT and digital industries. In Norway, women occupy just 28% of the tech jobs, and this percentage declines even more precipitously in entrepreneurship and leadership.

This contradiction raises pertinent questions. Why are there more women in tech in India, even with lower gender equality ratings? And why are the Nordics, with their liberal policies, so unable to encourage women to move into the sector? By examining both geographies, we can draw key lessons on how to enhance gender diversity in the world's technology sector. This part explores the structural, cultural, and policy-driven factors behind this divide.

Chapter 23
The Gender Divide in Tech

The contrast between India and the Nordic countries in female participation in the tech sector reveals a deeper, more complex narrative. While India accelerates ahead with increasing representation of women in IT, the Nordics—despite their reputation for equality—struggle to close the gender gap in tech leadership and entrepreneurship.

India's High Speed of Growth in Tech for Women

The major divergence lies in the support for entrepreneurs. The Invest India program assists women entrepreneurs in getting funded, connected, and incubated. For women entrepreneurs in tech in the Nordics, however, getting funded and scaling their business at the same speed as men is still challenging.

The other explanations for this achievement are closely related to India's larger digital transformation, government-backed inclusion efforts, and a change in professional goals among women culturally. India's IT sector has opened up well-structured opportunities for the career advancement of women, and this has been one major explanation for the sector's achievement. Infosys, Wipro, and TCS, big names in business, have brought on board mentorship schemes, leadership development programs, flexible working options, and anti-discrimination practices. India's strong emphasis on Mathematics in school curricula provides girls with a solid foundation to pursue careers in STEM. This early exposure to analytical and problem-solving skills has played a crucial role in increasing female representation in the tech sector.

Another significant change is because of remote and hybrid work patterns. These enable women to mix professional and domestic roles. The COVID-19 pandemic fast-tracked this change. Today, most businesses have persisted with flexible work arrangements. It has made it possible for women to be in the workplace while taking care of home duties.

The importance of role models in shaping gender diversity in IT cannot be understated. In Norway, many of the largest IT companies now have female CEOs, and initiatives like She Economy and Girl Tech Fest aim to create a more inclusive pipeline for women in tech. These programs recognize that change must happen at the systemic level—companies must adapt to diverse talent rather than expecting women to conform to traditional structures. As Hole Skogen from ICT Norway points out later in this part, diversity is not just an ethical imperative but a competitive advantage in fast-evolving industries like AI and cybersecurity.

In addition to Norway's initiatives, other Nordic countries have launched significant programs to enhance women's participation in technology. For instance, Women in Tech Sweden, a non-profit community with over 28,000 members, organizes Scandinavia's largest annual tech conference focused on women, providing networks and role models to inspire and support women in tech. Similarly, Finland leads the Action Coalition on Technology and Innovation for Gender Equality, part of the global Generation Equality campaign, focusing on preventing gender-based online violence and bridging the digital gender divide. Denmark has also been proactive; the Women to the

Top (W2T) project, which operated from 2003 to 2005, aimed to increase the number of women in top management positions through mentorship programs and networking, promoting gender equality in leadership roles.

The Indian state has also done its part by implementing initiatives such as Digital India and rural internet connectivity investments. It has offered unheard-of access to education and job opportunities, mainly for women working in second-tier cities and in rural regions. This assists in reframing women's employment opportunities.

Coding boot camps, online learning platforms, and focused skill development programs have helped more women shift into tech jobs. These initiatives have improved access to education and employment opportunities for women in second-tier cities and villages.

Another success story is CodingPro, an Indian education platform that initially had just 10-12% female students five years ago. Now the gender split has changed dramatically to 60% men and 40% women. With mobile-based learning, virtual mentorship, and placement support, CodingPro has enabled young women from disadvantaged backgrounds to join the tech industry.

It has been enabled through cutting-edge models of learning through which girls from rural areas have access to acquiring coding skills by using their mobile phones. Such initiatives have inbuilt inclusive support features in the form of 24/7 virtual tutoring, virtual guidance, intelligent tutors, adaptive technologies, efficient recording of attendance, and placement aid. Through technology-based platforms, CodingPro, among others, has facilitated pathways that make access to technical qualifications for women convenient, allowing them to obtain employable technical expertise in the digital economy. While India has made impressive progress, challenges remain.

Women in IT still face:

> ➤ Pay gaps compared to their male counterparts.

> ➤ Fewer promotions to senior roles, as men still dominate leadership positions.

> ➤ Cultural biases that discourage women from pursuing demanding careers.

> ➤ The burden of unpaid domestic labor limiting career growth.

> ➤ Workplace safety concerns and harassment.

This is where the Nordic model has lessons to impart. Nordic nations have excellent work-life balance policies, liberal parental leave, and strong legal safeguards against discrimination in the workplace. Indian businesses could incorporate similar policies to make sure that women not only join the tech industry but also excel in leadership positions.

The Nordic Paradox - Why Women Avoid Tech

Although they strongly believe in gender equality, the Nordics are challenged by women taking part in the tech sector. Tietoevry's recent survey reveals that fewer Nordic women would opt for education and a career in technology despite believing in the ability of technology to solve the greatest challenges the world is facing today, including climate change.

- In Finland, 66% of women think that technology can prevent climate change, but only 12% would venture into a tech career.

- Only 8% of women in Norway work in IT, although 45% think technology will solve the challenges facing the world.

- In Sweden, 26% of young women have been more interested in IT in the last three years, but interest in studying technology has decreased. Nevertheless, the sector is still viewed as non-inclusive, and interest in studying technology has decreased.

One of the biggest problems is the scarcity of female role models. Less than 10% of young women in the Nordics have a female mentor in IT. The IT industry remains masculine in character, and most women are not motivated to take up careers in the sector. The reasons behind this paradox are complex. One of the reasons is education and career counselling. Another is that the robust welfare frameworks and liberal parental leave policies, while providing invaluable support, have also served to reinforce traditional gender roles, as fewer women embark on careers in technology-driven industries. Most young women hold the opinion that schools and colleges do not do enough to encourage STEM (Science, Technology, Engineering, and Mathematics) among girls. There are fewer systematic attempts to prepare women for careers in STEM early on, which has further widened the gap.

Lastly, three in ten women say that tech businesses do not hire women actively. Family expectations also come into play. 44% of the women and 34% of the men feel that parents discourage their daughters from pursuing tech jobs. Most of the respondents consider the tech sector to be tough and male-dominated, with almost half of them feeling that increased inclusivity is needed to draw more women.

There are certain lessons that Nordics can learn from India. India's achievement in boosting women's participation in the IT sector is the result of systematic company policies, aggressive recruitment, and focused government initiatives. Indian firms have well-defined diversity targets, making sure that women are proactively recruited, educated, and advanced in the organization. This is where technology is perceived as a high-growth industry with good career opportunities. Invest India, a government initiative to encourage entrepreneurship and innovation, is another example of organized support systems promoting female leadership. Through special funding schemes, networking, and business incubators, Invest India has encouraged more women to become entrepreneurs in the technology sector.

How the Nordics Can Catch Up?

In the Nordics, women's lower presence in digital and IT sectors raises interesting questions concerning the efficacy of gender policy across various professional spheres. Even with robust anti-discrimination legislation and attempts at workplace diversity, most women in the Nordics continue to view technology as an uninviting or less desirable career option.

The absence of dedicated programs in the Nordics specifically aimed at breaking down the challenges women encounter in tech entrepreneurship has led to a slower pace of progress in spite of a general commitment to gender equality.

Norwegian NGOs like ICT Norway have also noted these challenges and are calling more forcefully for policies that would bring women into tech. Yet, much of that is still in the awareness stage, with fewer mass-scale interventions on the level of India's corporate-led inclusion drives.

Certain actions need to be taken by Nordic businesses and governments.

- Promoting early education in STEM subjects, engaging young girls via school initiatives.

- Developing more female role models in technology, highlighting successful women in the field.

- Adopting formal hiring and promotion policies like Indian IT companies.

- Investing in funding initiatives for women entrepreneurs in technology.

- Making the work environment more inclusive and making women feel at home in tech fields.

There are pathways in which both countries can take lessons from each other. The contrast between the Nordics and India serves to underscore the role of bespoke solutions to gender diversity in technology. This implies that while public policies can help establish a facilitative ecosystem for gender equality, specific sectoral interventions will be required to close gaps in sectors where women are underrepresented.

India's success is driven by company-led policies, online growth, and systematic skill-building. For instance, Wipro, a leading IT company in India, is an example of how policies of the corporate world can influence change. The gender inclusion strategies at Wipro involve mentorship, leadership training, and recruitment initiatives specifically targeted to bring in more women into all levels of the organization. By integrating diversity targets into its corporate framework, Wipro has been able to grow the number of women in management positions, showing that systematic private sector initiatives can bring measurable returns. This example might be a model for Nordic businesses to follow as they strive to fill their IT gender gaps.

Though the Nordics may have much to learn from the way India deals with gender diversity in technology, the converse also holds true. India continues to struggle with incidents of workplace harassment, safety issues, and strong cultural prejudices against women that check their professional ascension. The Nordic focus on work-life balance, good parental leave policies, and a broad culture of gender equality provides crucial lessons in maintaining long-term workplace gender equality. Indian businesses may learn from importing some aspects of the Nordic approach, including tougher legal safeguards against discrimination and better work-life integration, to be added to current initiatives.

The Nordics offer valuable lessons in work-life balance, parental leave, and long-term gender equality policies.

If Nordic countries adopt targeted recruitment efforts and India strengthens work-life policies and legal protections, both regions can create a more inclusive and diverse tech industry. By learning from each other, India and the Nordics can build a future where women participate in tech and lead in shaping the digital world.

Chapter 24

Sunita Mohanty on How India Is Leading in Gender Diversity in Tech

Sunita Mohanty, Senior VP and Chief Investment Officer at Invest India, has held leadership roles at Google Singapore. She has deep insights into India's success in gender diversity in tech. India has a rich legacy of women making it big in STEM, from Dr. Tessie Thomas in missile technology to Ritu Kurandar in space travel. Now, 43% of women join STEM and medicine for higher education, and 30% engage in the labor force. Socioeconomic considerations are behind this trend since STEM jobs promise stability, greater pay, and social status.

The Indian government has initiated major programs to help women in STEM. Vigyan Jyoti, a schoolgirl program for grades 9-12, has impacted 50,000 students by way of career guidance, science camps, and mentoring. WISE-KIRAN assists women in science and engineering through fellowships and research. The CURIE program enhances research infrastructure in women-only colleges and has impacted 42 colleges. STEM professions in India provide job security, higher pay, and work-life integration. Engineering and medicine are favoured professions, and children are pushed towards them early in life. Robust support systems within families, low costs for childcare, and domestic labor allow women to stay employed easily. Digital skill development programs prepare them further for technical and IT positions.

These efforts, along with corporate initiatives and online growth, have boosted the number of women in India's technology sector. Although India still has issues such as pay gaps and workplace prejudices, its methodical approach to inclusion provides important lessons for other nations, such as the Nordics.

Creating opportunities that are gender inclusive

Despite leading in gender equality, the Nordics struggle with female representation in tech leadership. India's structured approach—early intervention, role modelling, and societal support—offers valuable insights. One key learning strategy is involving both boys and girls in gender initiatives to create awareness and equal opportunities. It's interesting that India reaches out to girls in villages as early as ninth grade, unleashing huge talent. Even with Nordic leadership in gender equality, women's representation in tech is still a problem.

STEM is perceived as male-dominated and complex, which necessitates myth-busting and role modelling. Interventions should include girls and boys—girls require access, and boys need to learn about equality. Early sensitization helps to create an inclusive and supportive atmosphere for everyone. Career stability in the workplace is greatly sought after in India. STEM careers are viewed as secure, high-paid, and prestigious, with more work-life balance for women.

India's education system places a strong focus on math and science from a young age, with competitive exams leading to highly sought-after careers in engineering and medicine. One of the most important factors for women's success in STEM is the supportive environment—extended families, available domestic help, and parental support—allowing career advancement. This is different from Norway, where technology careers continue to grapple with old "nerd" stereotypes.

Shaped by a Pioneer

When asked, "Is there a woman in STEM or IT who has inspired your leadership journey? How do you relate to her story?" Sunita has a 24-year career in IT, banking, and the internet sector, and for 14 years, she worked in trust and safety at Google in product policies and online safety. She then moved to Invest India, enabling investors. An engineer by degree but with a marketing background, she has been curiosity- and risk-driven in her career. She celebrates both failure and success and learns from the former. Her early days were like those of many Indians who prioritize job security. But through the years, she developed strength, learning to take risks, fail quickly, and pivot—understanding that failure is but another step forward.

For Sunita, sponsorship and trust from mentors allowed her to be bold and take risks. Failure is hard, but after a long time, she has realized that a 40-year career is not marked by a small failure. Today, she counsels women to look at the long term, not a failed promotion or employment—these are merely small blips in a larger journey.

The woman who inspires her the most is her mother. She was Odisha's first female engineer. She studied engineering in a boys' college in 1965, residing in a medical hostel and cycling miles every day. Her story speaks volumes about the strength of will and the support of family. She then spent 20 years working for L&T as the sole lady engineer among men in a man's world. She did not fully understand her struggle when she was growing up, but her toughness defined her attitude. Due to this, she never felt like an outsider in a room full of men. She feels she belongs to the team, not as a woman.

She never prioritized her gender over her identity. She credits her mother's pioneering path as Odisha's first female engineer. Unlike most women who do not fit in male-dominated environments, she had grown up observing her mother being the only woman engineer at L&T for 20 years. Her profession, together with her father's, created a home where tasks were shared equally. This informed her that empowering women in STEM makes families stronger with intergenerational influence. Her parents' experience taught her that gender equality begins at home and has a lasting impact on her leadership and work environments today.

India has experienced great women leaders who have shaped her, other than her mother. Indira Gandhi, the first woman Prime Minister of India, exhibited tenacity and bold leadership in a patriarchal political environment. To this day, India still churns out inspirational women leaders in politics, business, and the sciences. In comparison to nations that are still grappling with female leadership, India has long accepted powerful women in leadership. Such icons reinforce the message that leadership is a matter of ability and not gender, and they continue to motivate Sunita to break boundaries and fight for participation in all arenas where she serves.

The Future of Women in Tech

Women in STEM and IT will experience growing success in the future. Women now have fresh leadership and innovation opportunities in emerging industries such as AI and quantum computing, as well as climate technology and biotechnology. Ritu Karidhal serves as an inspiring example for India as she designed the Mangalyaan and Chandrayaan 2 & 3 space missions that helped India become the first nation to accomplish its inaugural Mars mission successfully. Through her achievements, she shattered barriers faced by women in both aerospace engineering and space technology, thus proving that dedication and love of purpose lead to societal achievement.

STEM career availability has expanded for female candidates due to coronavirus-related changes such as virtual work environments and adaptable workplace designs, together with opportunities across international borders. Women now have unprecedented possibilities to create lasting impacts through the digital transformation of health tech, aerospace and sustainability sectors. Organizations now focus on greater diversity as well as leadership inclusion, which enhances the presence of women in executive roles. Nationwide regulations to impose female board members in corporate entities act as a key component to push for gender diversity.

Even with these advances, women remain hindered. Work evolution, automation, and fast technological progress render it hard to keep pace, particularly for those juggling family life. Unconscious AI, quantum computing, and other new technology biases result in underrepresentation. The pay gap exists, and bias in AI model training can reinforce disparities. Upskilling continuously and providing education that is accessible are essential to making women competitive in these technologies.

To maintain momentum, there is a need to invest in mentorship initiatives, inclusive policies, and skill development programs.

Empowering more young women to pursue STEM and equipping them with the appropriate resources will bridge the gender gap and build a more balanced future in technology and innovation.

Organizations need to take steps to enable sustainable gender diversity.

They are:

- Implement transparent hiring, equal pay, and merit-based promotions

- Provide leadership development, mentorship, and return-to-work programs

- Invest in unconscious bias training to create inclusive workplaces

- Hold leaders accountable for diversity objectives

- Culturally, sponsorship and mentorship are essential. Sponsors speak up for women's development in leadership, and mentorship builds skills and confidence. Sunita emphasises that mentors have been important in her career, speaking up for her in leadership meetings.

She provides some personal tips for women in STEM.

- Find mentors and sponsors- They will open doors and create opportunities.

- Lift as you climb – Support and uplift other women as you grow.

- Raise your hand for opportunities – Women often hesitate, thinking they're not ready. Step forward even if you feel unprepared.

The conversation highlights how India's structural efforts, role models, and corporate-government alliances have deepened the pipeline for women in STEM. Yet, consistent efforts in mentorship, policy support, and workplace inclusion continue to be essential. A special acknowledgement to Sunita for her insights and for sharing her mother's inspiring path—a reflection of strength and shattering of barriers. If women were able to do this 30–40 years ago, today's generation can very well keep the momentum going. Gender equality in STEM is not only a wish but a duty for everyone.

Chapter 25

Sunita Cherian on Lighthouse Leadership

Sunita Cherian, Chief Culture Officer and Senior Vice President –
Human Resources at Wipro Limited, has valuable perspectives on the
initiatives and strategies driving inclusivity in the industry. The DEI-
focused human capital management strategy at Wipro has benefited
from Sunita's important contribution. During her more than twenty-
year leadership, she transformed Wipro into an industry leader for DEI
which achieved worldwide recognition beyond India. Sunita served as
the Chair of NASSCOM's National D&I Council to promote inclusion
within Wipro and through the entire industry.

Wipro's DEI Recognition and Approach

Wipro achieved notable distinction through World Economic Forum recognition as a DEI Lighthouse due to its long-standing commitment toward placing inclusivity first. The Wipro certification confirms the company's dedication to building a workplace environment that promotes equal value for each employee and maximum performance across their full capability scope. Wipro stands out as a leader in IT diversity because its established inclusive culture results from core values that direct both business choices and organizational policy creation. An effective, multi-level structured diversity policy has been adopted by the organization, where programs are designed to go beyond mere tokenism and seek tangible change.

One of Wipro's star examples is the Women of Wipro initiative, launched in 2008, which supports women at various stages of their careers. From early career exposure and leadership development to flexible policies supporting caregiving needs, the company ensures that women are provided with the kind of support necessary to grow and thrive. These targeted initiatives have come a long way in positioning Wipro as a diversity leader in the international technology sector.

At Wipro, DEI is not a program, it is part of our organizational DNA. We are convinced that a diverse workforce generates innovation, enhances decision-making, and ultimately leads to better business outcomes. Sunita Cherian asserts that in Wipro, DEI is not corporate speak but an integral part of the business strategy. She cites that Wipro has embedded DEI in all stages of its operations, from recruitment and employee engagement to leadership development and decision-making. For instance, Wipro has established dedicated leadership programs that offer training and mentoring to women and diverse talent to propel their careers. Also, the organization's culture and policies are regularly fine-tuned to eliminate implicit bias and create a work environment in which every employee is made to feel valued and empowered.

Sunita Cherian explains how Wipro has structured its Diversity, Equity, and Inclusion (DEI) Council on a dual level—considering geographical and organizational pillars.[147] This serves to direct DEI strategies towards the distinct needs and population of specific regions, while staying aligned with the company's global vision. She identifies the stature and extent of Wipro and how the firm has over 220,000 employees spread globally in 60 countries and extending over 100 nationalities. Given this diverse global footprint, Wipro employees comprise individuals hailing from different backgrounds, ages, ethnicity, orientation, ability and cultures. This then creates a work environment with diverse generations, and perspectives. In most organizations, four to five generations in general tend to coexist under the same banner.

Making DEI More Than a Buzzword

Wipro has made deliberate choices by setting clear goals, tracking progress, and making leaders accountable.

Wipro has a DEI Council, led by our CEO, to ensure our diversity goals are tied to business success. Every business unit is responsible for its DEI performance, and we track key indicators to measure progress. One of the most significant is making leaders accountable. We ensure that leaders not only articulate DEI in speech but are involved in sponsorship, mentorship, and policy development.

Diversity is not an appendage; it is a foundational element of our team-building philosophy. Understanding that DEI cannot be left solely to the council, Wipro engages senior business leaders to lead initiatives at the leadership level. Sunita uses an example from real life—while constructing an account team to support a customer, diversity is a top preference. Because it sparks innovation and enhances customer success.

Apart from this, a group of inclusion leaders and employee resource groups (ERGs) has a critical role in making the DEI strategy real across business units and geographies. Rather than a standalone program, DEI is integrated into Wipro's business strategy, where it becomes second nature and organic to decision-making rather than forced dialogue.

Measuring Progress: The Role of KPIs in DEI

Sunita Cherian highlights that Wipro quantifies DEI success through a combination of quantitative and qualitative KPIs so that the improvement is thoroughly gauged. These metrics allow for measurement at different levels of the organization across representation, equity, and inclusion.[147] Through the examination of hiring, promotion, retention, leadership representation, and employee engagement data, Wipro can ensure that its DEI efforts are translated into concrete and measurable outcomes.

Along with numbers, qualitative metrics such as employee feedback, inclusion surveys, and cultural assessments provide insights into how diverse employees see the workplace. With data-driven practices, Wipro is in a position to continually fine-tune its strategies so that diversity and inclusion become an integral part of its business model.

Apart from this, DEI KPIs provide gender balance across various levels of leadership, underrepresented groups' retention rate and employee engagement scores to quantify workplace culture inclusivity. In addition to these, they quantify measures like unconscious bias in performance evaluations to provide equal career development opportunities to all employees.

Encouraging Women in Leadership

Sunita Cherian emphasizes that the advancement of women to leadership roles is a major strategy for Wipro. Systematic programs were initiated by the company to support women at different stages of their career. Mentorship schemes, leadership training sessions, sponsorship programs, and work-life balance policies are some of them.

Wipro also promotes gender diversity by creating a culture of skill enhancement, career growth, and leadership exposure. Wipro makes deliberate efforts to bridge the gender leadership gap. Sunita highlights that such efforts are not about creating representation but creating an inclusive environment where women can thrive and lead.

One of Sunita's favourite programs is ENRICH, a sponsorship program for high-potential women leaders. This is different from mentorship—sponsors are senior leaders who actively advocate for women's career growth, ensuring they receive leadership opportunities.[147]

Other key programs include:

- Inner Circle & Limitless: Focused on career development and leadership skills training.

- HerCode: A specialized program that enhances technical skills for women in tech.

- Wow Mom: An innovative program that empowers women before, during, and after maternity leave, so career progression is not disrupted by motherhood.

- Training programs for conscious career pathing at an associate level also helps employees match opportunities based on skill and aspiration.

These programs are not one-size-fits-all. Some are generic, while others are tailored to the needs of different geographies.

Changing Gender Norms Among Young Professionals

Sunita Cherian sees that even though conventional gender roles continue in India, there is a profound attitude shift between millennial and Gen Z professionals. Younger generations are becoming more stereoscopic and asking for greater gender balance while anticipating inclusive policies at work. In Wipro, this change comes in the form of a greater presence of women in STEM, leadership pipelines, and flexible work, as highlighted by Sunita. She underlines that newer-generation employees focus on diversity, equity, and inclusion (DEI) and encourage open talk about equal opportunity and fairness at workplaces. This change in thinking is driving change and creating inclusive and equitable workplaces.

Young men now share more in household work and childcare, especially in the city. Two-income families are now prevalent in the majority of industries. Wipro has provided paternity leave schemes and flexible work schedules to encourage a healthier balance in caregiving responsibilities.

Talent Development Program

The company actively implements special outreach programs, collaborates with diversity-focused recruitment partners, and uses equitable screening and selection processes. Additionally, initiatives like return ship programs for female return-to-work, internships for underrepresented groups, and training hiring managers in inclusive hiring help ensure a balanced hiring process. Diverse candidate slates to ensure gender balance in the hiring pipeline, bias training for hiring managers to eliminate unconscious bias, are some other initiatives they adopt. They also implement return ship programs, such as "Begin Again", to help women get back to work following career breaks.

AI and Data-Driven DEI Strategies

Wipro utilizes AI in the recruitment process to reduce biases in job postings, statistically screen resumes, and render impartial candidate evaluations. Analytical skills powered by AI help in tracking diversity measurements, gap detection, and providing input for more effective decision-making. AI is also used to support performance management so that unbiased promotions and appraisals are made through the analysis of patterns and identification of probable bias.

Further, Wipro employs AI to learn and develop, offering personalised career development recommendations to employees with diverse profiles. AI-powered chatbots and employee feedback mechanisms also facilitate inclusivity by allowing employees to report issues and gain support in real time.

Sunita highlights that AI, when used in a responsible manner, is a robust enabler to make workplaces more inclusive and support Wipro's diversity and equity commitments at all levels.

- Examine gender compensation imbalances and recommend adjustments.

- Identify bias within job advertisements, utilizing inclusive terminology.

- Track real-time DEI measures through customized dashboards.

Collaboration with Clients on DEI

Sunita Cherian tells us Wipro actively involves customers to exchange diversity and equality best practices through knowledge-sharing platforms and benchmarking research while providing strategic solutions and executable options that enhance DEI programs. Such collaborative engagements enable businesses to benefit from Wipro's specialized expertise through adopting good policies, which helps them establish sustainable diversity frameworks. Knowledge sharing among businesses promotes universal workplace development, leading to equal treatment for all staff members worldwide.

The company receives repeated requests from customers to help them establish their own Diversity, Equity, and Inclusion (DEI) programs. Through co-development programs, Wipro supports organisations by jointly conducting DEI workshops as well as benchmarking studies that help these organisations implement effective, sustainable diversity practices.

Lessons for the Nordics from India's IT Sector

In India, the tech sector has encouraged women's talent actively through systematic policies, skill development initiatives, and effective leadership accountability. Nordic businesses can benefit by adopting detailed sponsorship programs and early-stage mentorship programs to increase gender inclusion in tech.

Chapter 26

Mali Hole Skogen on Tech, Diversity, and Change

Mali Hole Skogen, Director at ICT Norway, explores gender diversity in the Nordic IT sector and its comparison to India's advancements. Drawing from her extensive industry experience, she sheds light on the challenges and opportunities for women in tech, particularly in Norway and the broader Nordic region.

An overview of gender diversity in Norway's IT industry

Currently, women make up 31% of Norway's tech industry, with growth in recent years, especially in university enrolments. Over half of the increase in IT studies in the past decade is due to women, giving hope for further progress. However, the number of women in leadership has declined from 34% to 27% in five years, a concerning trend we aim to understand and address. According to Statistics Norway, there are currently around 7,000 managers in the Norwegian IT sector, and around 1,000 of these are women. On the other hand, the IT industry is the sector in Norway with the lowest wage gap between women and men at all levels. We also have some outliers in our data due to COVID-19 and other factors. However, we are committed to identifying the root causes and making necessary changes as soon as possible.

Sector-wise, fewer women are in STEM-heavy fields like software and hardware. We also feel they are reducing in telecom and consultancies. The numbers are similar across Nordic countries, with Sweden slightly ahead. We observe that in the more technical areas of IT, where STEM courses and expertise are essential, men significantly outnumber women. Efforts to inspire girls to pursue tech are ongoing, and IT's integration into medicine, biology, and AI may attract more women into tech-related roles outside the traditional IT industry.

Challenges in achieving better gender balance

Despite various initiatives, increasing female leadership remains a challenge. Role models play a key role in inspiring more women to enter and stay in IT leadership. According to Mali Hole Skogen, the numbers in tech are the same in all the Nordic countries except Sweden. Denmark faces a similar situation, highlighting a common challenge which needs to be addressed. These dynamics could positively impact diversity in the IT sector.

In Norway, many of the largest IT companies now have female CEOs, a relatively new but encouraging development. Mali Hole Skogen emphasizes the power of female leadership, as women are inspired by other women to pursue leadership roles and IT studies. Strong role models help change perceptions and create opportunities for other people. She explains that there is a longstanding history of women participating within the workforce and taking on leadership positions. This was exemplified at the event ICT Norway organized, where women political leaders met women IT managers to discuss what similarities there were in the politics and business worlds.

She draws an interesting parallel to Norwegian politics. In 1981, the country's first female Prime Minister, Gro Harlem Brundtland, took office. This was a milestone that opened doors for more women in power. Since then, a number of political party leaders and Prime Ministers have been women. The IT sector may also follow a similar pattern, with women proving that it is possible to shatter the glass ceiling. This shift is also reflected in the broader Nordic society. With more women stepping into leadership roles in both politics and IT, it is evident that change has already begun.

Concerning the Nordic region, gender balance within leadership has greatly improved, as Finland and Sweden have had female Prime Ministers. Norway is also experiencing a rise in the number of women in leadership positions, such as Anita Krohn Traaseth, former CEO of Innovation Norway. Mali Hole Skogen emphasizes how having women in executive roles motivates aspiring female candidates to take up engineering and other technical disciplines, which has an empowering effect.

When asked about programs and policies that have transformed the Nordic IT sector in terms of diversity, she referred to several initiatives that seek to attract young women with an interest in technology. Looking back to her university days, she remembers that the distribution of students by gender was not equal for all scientific branches. Biology had a predominance of women, while astrophysics, physics, and higher-level mathematics had a predominately male demographic. However, as more and more women entered these previously male-dominated professions, they encouraged other women to join as well.

A similar trend is evident in medicine, which, despite being a rigorous natural science field, is now dominated by women in Norway. So much emphasis is placed on the issues of gender balance in medical schools that faculties are actually addressing concerns. This proves the point that diversity breeds diversity; for example, women who perceive their field as representing them are more likely to feel as though their participation will enrich the discussions, debates, and overall learning process. As Mali Hole Skogen pointed out, it is crucial to build spaces where people feel invited rather than excluded. No matter whether it is the classroom or the office, instilling a sense of belonging encourages full participation from both men and women. This tenet has influenced her personal development while working in the industry and is what many of her colleagues are now trying to embrace.

Reflecting on history, today's women in tech and management are still breaking down barriers. The women who preceded them had to be truly remarkable to even have access to male-dominated careers. Reflecting on history now in 2025, it is difficult to envision what life was like a hundred years ago to be one of the first female engineers, judges, or physicians. Women have only had about 100 to 150 years to enter historically male-dominated careers, so their progress is fairly recent.

People such as Marie Curie in chemistry and Gro Harlem Brundtland in politics weren't only talented—they needed to be great to be taken seriously. Most of the women who contributed to the greatest scientific and intellectual achievements went unrecognized, toiling in the shadows of their male peers. Their persistence, tenacity, and determination laid the groundwork for the doors women have opened today. Acknowledging their efforts is essential in realizing how far gender equality has progressed—and how much farther it must go.

We've heard many stories about women who played crucial roles behind the scenes, supporting Nobel Prize winners and other pioneers without receiving the recognition they deserved. There are so many untold contributions in these "grey zones" of history. These women not only had to be brilliant but also needed extraordinary resilience, perseverance, and willpower to navigate environments where they were constantly marginalized. It's a testament to their strength and determination that they pushed forward despite these barriers.

Diversity as a Driver of Innovation in a Volatile Tech Landscape

Mali Hole Skogen shares her admiration for Norway's IT sector, highlighting the intelligence and innovation that define the industry. Having spoken with many female leaders, she notes that their paths to leadership vary widely, often shaped by unexpected challenges and personal motivations. These stories reveal both common bottlenecks—such as salary gaps and family responsibilities—and unique struggles that shaped their careers. She believes such experiences deserve more attention, perhaps even as a dedicated podcast series featuring women who have navigated their way to C-level positions. When asked how companies can align diversity goals with business outcomes, she points to an intriguing debate ahead of International Women's Day. ICT Norway has collaborated with major tech companies like Google, Microsoft, and Meta on AI studies comparing the Nordic IT sector to global trends. A key finding in multiple reports suggests a strong correlation between companies with a defined AI strategy and diverse leadership teams.

The reason behind this link remains unclear—whether diversity drives innovation in AI or whether AI-driven companies naturally attract diverse talent. However, given the consistency of this finding across studies, she believes further research is necessary. She also notes that IT is a volatile industry where adaptability and broad perspectives are crucial. In this context, diverse leadership may be a key factor in staying competitive and fostering innovation.

Mali Hole Skogen reflects on the rapid changes that have shaped the IT industry in Norway over the past five years. When she entered the industry for the first time, the COVID-19 pandemic spurred digitalization at an unprecedented rate. Companies were forced to adapt in a hurry, and the IT sector experienced gigantic growth both in Norway and worldwide. Just as the industry was getting used to this digital change, the large-scale invasion of Ukraine put cybersecurity and digital war in the spotlight. The need to protect digital infrastructures became more apparent than ever.

Then came another major shift—the launch of ChatGPT-4, which democratized AI by making powerful tools accessible to the general public. This revolutionized industries worldwide, changing how people interacted with technology. She sees these events as markers of just how volatile the IT industry is. Success in this field requires companies to adapt quickly, seize new opportunities, and innovate continuously. Interestingly, a survey shows that there is a high correlation between firms with a clear AI strategy and firms with diverse leadership groups. She posits that diversity in leadership integrates people with various backgrounds, skills, and viewpoints—a critical benefit when industries experience sudden changes. The diverse group is better positioned to address impromptu change, be it the advent of new technologies, global emergencies, or changes in consumer needs.

She compares this flexibility with the German automobile sector, which, for many years, rode on a homogeneous team of engineers educated in the same schools. When electric cars shook the industry, most German automakers were unable to turn around in time. This case highlights the need for varied expertise in handling technological changes. In IT, especially with AI, diverse leadership companies are in a better place to innovate and stay ahead.

She also observes that Indian managers top the management teams of several of the world's biggest tech companies, such as Microsoft and Google. It could partially be because they were successful in forming teams that were diversified but very skilled. Progress is believed to be best brought about through collaboration with others who have different experiences and backgrounds, an idea now accepted as an integral force driving innovation. In Norway, different initiatives have been started to ensure gender diversity in the fields of IT and finance. She emphasizes programs like ODA, She economy, and Girl Tech Fest, which help to promote the participation of women in tech fields. Girl Tech Fest, for instance, familiarizes young girls with coding in a fun and interactive manner, expanding their scope of what it means to work in tech.

Another influential initiative is She economy, which engages CEOs of Norway's biggest technology firms, such as Google and Microsoft, along with academics and the military. The community provides a forum for women to discuss female leadership in the IT and financial industries, leading to crucial conversations at the uppermost level. One of She economy's standout programs is its annual study trip to Silicon Valley, held at Googleplex. The event gathers professors from Stanford, top industry leaders, and women in tech for four days of learning, networking, and collaboration.

What is novel about the She Economy is its philosophy: "Change the system, not the women." Instead of asking women to fit into current structures, the effort is trying to transform the corporate space to be more accommodating. It brings to the fore how companies can gain from diversity not as a moral imperative but as a business strength that creates adaptability and agility. Mali's observations provide insight into the changing dynamics of the IT industry and the significance of leadership diversity in overcoming technology disruptions. Norway's experience is a lesson to businesses globally, including in India, to cultivate more inclusive spaces that lead to long-term prosperity.

Mali stresses that women do not need to adapt to suit male-dominated leadership positions—the system must be altered. This perspective is central to initiatives like She Economy, which encourages diversity in leadership. She highlights its Silicon Valley study trips, where women from the Nordics and beyond gather at Googleplex for discussions with top industry leaders. Her own experience on this trip led to lasting friendships and invaluable insights.

A Call to Strengthen Norway's IT Talent Pipeline

Shifting focus to Norway's IT talent pipeline, she expresses concern over the limited number of IT study places. Currently, Norway offers 3,000 IT study spots annually, while over 18,000 students apply. This stark imbalance has persisted despite ICT Norway's efforts to push for more opportunities. The Norwegian government reports a higher figure—around 8,000—by including media-related studies, but the core IT programs remain insufficient.

A major issue is the concentration of IT talent in just 25–30 large companies, which offer competitive salaries and attractive work environments. As a result, few graduates pursue careers in academia or the public sector, creating a talent gap in research and government institutions. This lack of IT expertise in the public sector forces reliance on expensive consultancy firms, raising concerns about Norway's ability to navigate the AI-driven industrial revolution.

She argues that for a sustainable democracy, scientific knowledge and expertise should be more evenly distributed. She sees the high demand for IT education as an opportunity to strengthen Norway's talent base, but political prioritization is lacking. Unlike India, which has invested heavily in IT education, Norway's slow response has left it trailing behind in developing a robust and diverse tech workforce.

The lack of IT talent and volume in Norway is a growing concern. Over 90% of IT graduates from Norwegian universities end up working for the same 25-30 large companies which dominate the sector by offering high salaries and attractive work environments. This concentration of talent limits the growth of university research and the public sector, which struggles to retain skilled professionals. As a result, the government increasingly relies on costly consultants from major firms, raising concerns about knowledge distribution and long-term sustainability.

Norway's university IT environments, while strong, remain too small. This highlights a significant untapped potential in young talent eager to enter the field. Expanding IT education would help balance the talent distribution across academia, the private sector, and public institutions, ensuring broader expertise in emerging fields like artificial intelligence and data science.

In today's rapidly evolving digital landscape, a strong university sector is critical for recruiting and nurturing talent, fostering innovation, and supporting democracy through scientific advancement. However, IT education has not been a political priority for a long time, leading to an imbalanced labor market where private companies absorb most of the available talent.

Some Norwegian IT firms, particularly those competing globally, recruit talent internationally rather than from local universities. This creates a two-tier system: Traditional consultancies and industry giants dominate local hiring, while global players seek expertise beyond Norway's borders. The lack of investment in higher education and research leaves the country lagging behind tech powerhouses like India, where IT education and workforce development have been prioritized.

To strengthen Norway's IT sector and create a more balanced, future-proof economy, expanding university IT programs and fostering research environments should be a national priority.

Global Inspiration and Personal Commitment to Change

Mali Hole Skogen emphasizes that women shouldn't have to change to fit leadership roles—the system must change. She highlights Economy and Silicon Valley study trips that empower women in tech. Norway's IT talent shortage is a major concern. Most graduates join a handful of large companies, leaving academia and the public sector struggling to retain IT talent. This imbalance threatens innovation and the country's ability to compete in an AI-driven world.

She encourages global talent, including from India, to consider Norway, highlighting strong salaries and work-life balance. She notes that IT careers provide financial independence, opening opportunities for women. Comparing India's higher female participation in IT (nearing 40%), she urges the Nordics to foster inclusive ecosystems.

She stresses the value of diverse teams, innovation through collaboration, and strengthening democracy with tech literacy. Personally, she promotes STEM education at home, making math and coding fun for children. Her key message: embrace diverse perspectives and support IT education to drive gender equality and economic growth.

Epilogue

The relationship between India and the Nordics exemplifies this spirit. What started as diplomatic ties has grown into a partnership of shared ambitions focused on sustainability, innovation, and equality. Each region serves as a mirror for the other—one reflecting untapped potential and the other presenting a model for inclusive growth. The Nordic nations have established societies where gender equality is ingrained in policy and culture. At the same time, India, with its vast and dynamic workforce, demonstrates that inclusion can thrive despite systemic challenges. Their collaboration is not merely an exchange of ideas but a blueprint for a future where economic growth and gender equity go hand in hand.

But change is never passive; it demands action. As readers, leaders, and changemakers, we bear the responsibility of fostering a more inclusive world. The stories in this book are more than just narratives—they are calls to action.

The Third India-Nordic Summit, set to take place in Norway in May 2025, marks a significant chapter in India-Nordic relations and stands as a powerful symbol of our shared future. As the Nordic Prime Ministers and Prime Minister Narendra Modi come together to reaffirm their commitments, we are reminded that true progress is a dynamic, ongoing process—one that flourishes through collaboration and collective action across all sectors of society.

To have this book launched during our India-Nordic Business Week is a deliberate effort to ensure that the gender agenda and Nari Shakti—women's empowerment—are firmly embedded in the India-Nordic dialogue. We are grateful to the Nordic Council of Ministers for making this important publication possible.

In alignment with this commitment to global collaboration, Det Moderne India is co-hosting the India-Nordic Business Week in partnership with the Indian Danish Chamber of Commerce, Sweden-India Business Council, India Nordic Water Forum, Confederation of Indian Industry, Ernst & Young, and The Conduit. As part of this initiative, we will also convene an India-Nordic Roundtable—continuing the dialogue that began with the Indo-Nordic Cooperation Seminar at The International Climate Summit 2023, then the roundtable at Davos, and deepened through engagements in India.

The stories in this book highlight the courage and perseverance of those who have shattered barriers, but real change requires collective effort. Whether you are a business leader, policymaker, educator, or ally, you have the power to challenge biases, mentor future leaders, and advocate for more inclusive policies. Gender equity is not just a moral imperative—it is an economic and social necessity. The future depends on those willing to act today.

This book is not a conclusion—it is a call to shape industries, communities, and mindsets in ways that honor those who paved the way and empower those who will follow. The journey toward equality and innovation is ongoing, and as history has shown us, The First and Only never remain alone for long.

Acknowledgements

The First and Only would not have been possible without the guidance, support, and inspiration of so many along the way.

To the founders of Det Moderne India (DMI)—thank you for your pioneering spirit and your determination to create a platform that bridges India, Norway, and the Nordics.

To DMI's podcast guests, members, partners, and contributors—thank you for generously sharing your insights, experiences, and vision. Your courage and resilience are the foundation of this book, and I am truly honored to share your journeys.

A heartfelt thank you to the Indian-Danish Chamber of Commerce, the Sweden-India Business Council, and Invest India for fostering invaluable collaborations that continue to strengthen India-Nordic relations. Hosting a roundtable at the World Economic Forum in Davos in 2023—when DMI was barely two years old—was a defining moment that firmly put us on the map.

To the incredible men I have met as mentors, bosses, supporters, and friends—your encouragement and belief in me have shaped my journey in ways beyond words.

A special thank you to the board of DMI and Erik Solheim, Per Morten Hoff, Tone Helleland Johnsen, Ganesh Shenoy and Atle Vidar

Nagel Johansen for your invaluable contributions to shaping Det Moderne India into what it is today.

Technology can be a powerful tool, and AI played a helpful role in refining ideas and enhancing clarity during the early stages of this book.

I am indebted to the many women and men who generously shared their thoughts and reflections throughout the writing process: Karin Berle Gabrielsen, Stig Traavik, Grethe Heide Arnesen, Hanne Va, Victor Yash Klippgen, Håvard Hugås, Rachel Wilson Rugelsjøen, Jyoti Sohal-David, Einar Ravndal, Michelle Chinnappen, Knut Godager, my former editor Knut André Karlstad, and psychologist Nina Bråten.

My gratitude also goes to my teachers, Trygve Hval Andersen and Torgeir Thunselle, who believed in me. Your encouragement ignited a hunger for knowledge and gave me the confidence to pursue it. The way you upgraded my grades based on my debating skills probably laid the foundation for everything that followed. That drive led me to a moment my 17-year-old self had only dared to dream of—greeting Indian Prime Minister Modi at the launch of the Indian TV channel NewsX World. Who would have thought, back then, that such a moment would come?

Dearest Nikki Bhabhi—look at life and look back. Thank you for being my rock in my pursuit of freedom—for being that effortlessly cool tomboy, full of laughter, curiosity, and a zest for life. *Kya innocent zamane the.*

Arman—thank you for your dedication and your willingness to find solutions. To my daughters, Aditi and Sushmita—I have watched you grow into the grounded, humble, and extraordinary young women you are today. You carry the future in your hands and I am blessed to follow you.

Acknowledgements

Though my relationship with my parents was far from easy, I acknowledge with gratitude the most enduring gift they gave me: India. Its language, culture, and spirit have always remained with me. My parents left India in the 1970s, carrying the richness of their heritage and the hope of building a better future in Norway. They worked tirelessly between these two worlds—India and Norway—to create new opportunities for the next generations. From them, I inherited the values of modesty and frugality, the importance of hard work, and honesty. These values have shaped who I am and continue to guide me.

To my brother Ravi—the *first and only* in his own right. Though we walk separate paths today, I respect the way you sacrificed yourself to fulfill our parents' dreams. You worked every day after school, shouldering burdens that were never fairly shared among us siblings. While I chose a different path, I honor all that you gave to the family.

And last, but certainly not least—Morten. You have lifted me when I could not stand and given me the wings to soar when I doubted my own strength. If there is such a thing as future lives, I hope I will be yours in all of them.

Published by Det Moderne India

This book is part of our ongoing mission to amplify voices that shape a more inclusive and sustainable future between India and the Nordics.

References

Endnotes

1. Nordic Council of Ministers, *The Nordic Region – Strong Economies and Shared Values* (Copenhagen: Nordic Council of Ministers, 2022), https://www.norden.org/en/publication/nordic-region-strong-economies-and-shared-values.

2. The Common Nordic Labour Market – 70 Years and Beyond." *Nordregio*, 2024. https://pub.nordregio.org/r-2024-14-nordic-labour-market-70-years/1-introduction.html

3. Nordic Council of Ministers. *The Nordic Region – Strong Economies and Shared Values.* Copenhagen: Nordic Council of Ministers, 2022. https://www.norden.org/en/publication/nordic-region-strong-economies-and-shared-values.

4. Nordregio. "The Common Nordic Labour Market – 70 Years and Beyond." *Nordregio*, 2024. https://pub.nordregio.org/r-2024-14-nordic-labour-market-70-years/1-introduction.html.

5. The Global Economy.com. "Norway: Female Labor Force Participation." Last modified 2023. https://www.theglobaleconomy.com/Norway/Female_labor_force_participation/

6. Global People Strategist. *7 Countries with the Best Paternity Leave Policies*. Accessed March 22, 2025. https://globalpeoplestrategist.com/7-countries-with-the-best-paternity-leave/

7. Nordic Council of Ministers, *Work–Life Balance the Nordic Way* (Copenhagen: Nordic Council of Ministers, 2020), https://www.norden.org/en/information/work-life-balance-nordic-way

8. Nordic Labour Journal, "Four Nordic Women Prime Ministers at the Same Time," *Nordic Labour Journal*, November 29, 2021, https://www.nordiclabourjournal.org/nyheter/news-2021/article.2021-11-29.1160864634.

9. Nordic Cooperation. "Women in Nordic Politics: A Continuing Tradition." Accessed March 22, 2025. https://www.norden.org/en/news/women-nordic-politics-continuing-tradition

10. Nordic Council of Ministers, *Nordic Co-operation: Facts about the Nordic Region*, Copenhagen: Nordic Council of Ministers, 2022, https://www.norden.org/en/information/nordic-co-operation

11. Anna Lazarus Caplan, "European Country Named Happiest for Eighth Year in a Row — Where Does the U.S. Rank?" *People*, March 20, 2024, https://people.com/european-country-named-happiest-for-eighth-year-where-does-us-rank-11700287

12. Moneycontrol, "India's GDP Doubles in a Decade, Poised to Overtake Japan in 2025, Germany by 2027," last modified March 22, 2025, https://www.moneycontrol.com/news/india/india-s-gdp-doubles-in-a-decade-poised-to-overtake-japan-in-2025-germany-by-2027-12972326.html

13. Central Intelligence Agency, *The World Factbook: GDP (Purchasing Power Parity) – Country Comparison*, accessed March 22, 2025, https://www.cia.gov/the-world-factbook/field/real-gdp-purchasing-power-parity/country-comparison/

14. Worldometer, "India Population (2024)," accessed March 22, 2025, https://www.worldometers.info/world-population/india-population/

15. Dipanjan Roy Chaudhury, "India's Gen Z Is 377 Million Strong, the Largest Ever in the Country," *The Economic Times*, August 11, 2023, https://economictimes.indiatimes.com/news/india/indias-gen-z-is-377-million-strong-the-largest-ever-in-the-country/articleshow/102601367.cms

16. United Nations, "UN Founding Members," accessed March 22, 2025, https://research.un.org/en/unmembers/founders

17. United Nations Secretary-General, "Secretary-General's Remarks on the Partnership Between India and the United Nations at India's 75th Anniversary," October 19, 2022, https://www.un.org/sg/en/content/sg/speeches/2022-10-19/secretary-generals-remarks-the-partnership-between-india-and-the-united-nations-india%E2%80%99s-75th-anniversary

18. Ashley J. Tellis, "India in the Emerging World Order," *Carnegie Endowment for International Peace*, November 6, 2023, https://carnegieendowment.org/2023/11/06/india-in-emerging-world-order-pub-90928.

19. *Diplomatist*, "Global Leadership in Sustainability: India's Role in the International Solar Alliance and Climate-Resilient Infrastructure," November 30, 2024, https://diplomatist.com/2024/11/30/global-leadership-in-sustainability-indias-role-in-the-international-solar-alliance-and-climate-resilient-infrastructure/

20.   All India Council for Technical Education (AICTE), "Ancient Universities in India," accessed March 22, 2025, https://www.aicte-india.org/downloads/ancient.pdf

21.   Government of India, *Census of India 2011: Language*, Office of the Registrar General & Census Commissioner, accessed March 22, 2025, https://censusindia.gov.in/census.website/data/census-2011/language

22.   Federation of Indian Chambers of Commerce and Industry (FICCI), "Indian Media and Entertainment Industry Clocks 13% Growth to Reach INR 1.67 Trillion in 2018," March 12, 2019, https://ficci.in/press_release_details/3374

23.   Statista, "Number of Eligible Voters in India as of January 2024," accessed March 22, 2025, https://www.statista.com/statistics/1446212/india-number-of-eligible-voters/

24.   Ministry of External Affairs, Government of India. "Joint Press Statement from the Summit between India and the Nordic Countries," 2018. https://www.mea.gov.in/bilateral-documents.htm?dtl/29828/.

25.   Ministry of External Affairs, Government of India, *India-Nordic Summit: Stockholm 2018 – Joint Statement*, May 2018, https://www.mea.gov.in/bilateral-documents.htm?dtl/29853/IndiaNordic_Summit_Stockholm_Joint_Statement_May_2018

26.   Ministry of External Affairs, Government of India, *2nd India-Nordic Summit: Joint Statement*, May 4, 2022, https://www.mea.gov.in/press-releases.htm?dtl/35277/2nd_IndiaNordic_Summit.

27.   Ministry of Commerce & Industry, Government of India, "India-European Free Trade Association Sign Trade and Economic Partnership Agreement," *Press Information Bureau*,

March 10, 2024, https://pib.gov.in/PressReleasePage.aspx?PRID=2013169

28. India Briefing. (2024, September 23). *A Promising Future for India-Finland Collaboration*. India Briefing News. https://www.india-briefing.com/news/a-promising-future-for-india-finland-collaboration-34562.html/

29. Rao, Archana. "India-Norway Trade and Investment Relations." India Briefing News, October 9, 2024. https://www.india-briefing.com/news/india-norway-trade-and-investment-relations-34704.html/.

30. Jensen, Carsten. *Equality in the Nordic World*. University of Wisconsin Pres, 2021.

31. Larsen, Eirinn, Ulla Manns, and Ann-Catrin Östman. "Gender-Equality Pioneering, or How Three Nordic States Celebrated 100 Years of Women's Suffrage." *Scandinavian Journal of History* 47, no. 5 (January 25, 2022): 624–47. https://doi.org/10.1080/03468755.2021.2023035.

32. Stevenson, Betsey. "The Impact of Divorce Laws on Marriage-Specific Capital." *Journal of Labor Economics* 25, no. 1 (December 18, 2006): 75–94. https://doi.org/10.1086/508732.

33. Nordic Council of Ministers, *Gender Equality in the Nordic Labour Market: Women in STEM*, accessed March 22, 2025, https://www.norden.org/en/statistics/education.

34. Our World In Data, "Female Labor Force Participation Rate," accessed March 22, 2025, https://ourworldindata.org/female-labor-supply

35. Gupta, Nabanita Datta, Nina Smith, and Mette Verner. "Child Care and Parental Leave in the Nordic Countries:

A Model to Aspire To?" *SSRN Electronic Journal*, January 1, 2006. https://doi.org/10.2139/ssrn.890298.

36. Nordic Council of Ministers, *Nordic Gender Equality in Figures 2021*, accessed March 22, 2025, https://www.norden.org/en/publication/nordic-gender-equality-figures-2021.

37. BBC News, "The Day Iceland's Women Went on Strike," *BBC World Service*, October 24, 2020, https://www.bbc.com/news/world-europe-34640382.

38. World Economic Forum. "Global Gender Gap Report 2024," 2024. https://www.weforum.org/publications/global-gender-gap-report-2024/in-full/economic-and-leadership-gaps-constraining-growth-and-skewing-transitions-7b05a512cb/.

39. McKinsey Global Institute, "The Role of Women in Driving Economic Growth: A Global Perspective," accessed March 22, 2025, https://www.researchgate.net/publication/383580905_The_Role_of_Women_in_Driving_Economic_Growth_A_Global_Perspective

40. Nordic Statistics, "All-time low Nordic fertility rates," accessed March 22, 2025, https://www.nordicstatistics.org/news/all-time-low-nordic-fertility-rates/

41. Government of India, *The Hindu Succession (Amendment) Act, 2005*, Ministry of Law and Justice, https://legislative.gov.in/actsofparliamentfromtheyear/hindu-succession-amendment-act-2005

42. BBC News, "More Indian Women Keeping Their Maiden Names after Marriage," *BBC News*, March 12, 2022, https://www.bbc.com/news/world-asia-india-60682832

43. International Labour Organization, *India: Female Labour Force Participation Rate*, accessed March 22, 2025, https://ilostat.ilo.org/data/.

44. Mehta, Rini Bhattacharya. "Gender and Modernity in Indian Cinema: *Queen* and the New Female Narrative." *South Asian Popular Culture* 18, no. 1 (2020): 23–35. https://doi.org/10.1080/14746689.2020.1712081.

45. Rachel Dwyer, *Bollywood's India: Hindi Cinema as a Guide to Contemporary India* (London: Reaktion Books, 2014)

46. Great Place to Work Institute, *Unmasking the Gender Disparity in Indian Leadership: A Compelling Imperative for Transformation*, accessed March 22, 2025, https://www.greatplacetowork.in/unmasking-the-gender-disparity-in-indian-leadership-a-compelling-imperative-for-transformation.

47. UNICEF India, *Gender Equality*, accessed March 22, 2025, https://www.unicef.org/india/what-we-do/gender-equality.

48. National Institute on Aging, *Education and Gender Inequality May Explain Why India's Women Have Worse Late-Life Cognition*, accessed March 22, 2025, https://www.nia.nih.gov/news/education-and-gender-inequality-may-explain-why-indias-women-have-worse-late-life-cognition

49. Arora, S. 2024. "Policy and Societal Change." Interview by R. Sunder. *Det Moderne India's Podcast.* Accessed March 27, 2025. https://www.dmi.no

50. Arora, S. 2024. "Challenges in Recruiting Women in India Podcast Series—HR Practices and Company Level Challenges Part-2." Interview by R. Sunder. *Det Moderne India's Podcast,* no. 63. Accessed March 28, 2025. https://www.dmi.no

51. Strachan, Glenda, and Arosha S Adikaram. "Women's Work in South Asia: Reflections on the Past Decade." *South Asian Journal of Human Resources Management* 10, no. 2 (October 6, 2023): 244–55. https://doi.org/10.1177/23220937231198381.

52. Ramoso, Zarah Denese, and Guzyal Hill. *Balancing Work and New Parenthood: A Comparative Analysis of Parental Leave in Australia, Canada, Germany and Sweden.* Anthem Press, 2023.

53. Poonia, Astha. "Sexual harassment at workplace." *Amity International Journal of Juridical Sciences* 5, no. 1 (2019): 50-60.

54. Profeta, Paola, Maria Lucia Passador, and Ximena Caló. "Reporting Obligations Regarding Gender Equality and Equal Pay." *Bocconi Legal Studies Research Paper* 3953710 (2021).

55. Ghosal, Abhijeet. "Role of Panchayati Raj Institutions for Empowerment of Disabled Person with the Perspective of Census of India, 2011."

56. Aimsinternational.com. "Women's Leadership in FMCG: Driving Innovation & Inclusion," 2025. https://www.aimsinternational.com/news/women-s-leadership-in-fmcg-a-driving-force-for-innovation-and-inclusion.

57. Ciifoundation.in. "Woman Exemplar Program," 2024. https://ciifoundation.in/wep.php.

58. fundsforNGOs. "CII Foundation Announces Woman Exemplar Award (India) - FundsforNGOs." fundsforNGOs - Grants and Resources for Sustainability, July 21, 2022. https://www2.fundsforngos.org/social-service/cii-foundation-announces-woman-exemplar-award-india/.

59. Sunder, Rina. "Det Moderne India (E-Bok)." Gyldendal. no, 2019. https://www.gyldendal.no/faglitteratur/e-boeker/oekonomi-og-administrasjon/det-moderne-india-(e-bok)/p-10024791-no/.

60. Tewari, Trisha. "Fresher Jobs for Women Soar by 48% in India, but Leadership Still Elusive, Says Report: Is Corporate Glass Ceiling the Culprit?" The Times of India. Times Of India, March 24, 2025. https://timesofindia.indiatimes.com/education/news/fresher-jobs-for-women-soar-48-in-india-but-leadership-still-elusive-says-report-is-corporate-glass-ceiling-the-culprit/articleshow/119416545.cms.

61. Kumar, R. 2024. "Challenges in Recruiting Women in India Podcast Series—HR Practices and Company-Level Challenges Part-1." Interview by R. Sunder. *Det Moderne India's Podcast*, no. 62. Accessed March 28, 2025. https://www.dmi.no

62. Kumar, R. 2024. "HR Practices and Company-Level Challenges." Interview by R. Sunder. *Det Moderne India's Podcast*. Accessed March 27, 2025. https://www.dmi.no

63. Mishra, S. 2025. "What Women Want." Interview by R. Sunder. *Det Moderne India's Podcast*. Accessed March 27, 2025. https://www.dmi.no

64. Mishra, S. 2024. "Challenges in Recruiting Women in India Podcast Series—What Women Want?" Interview by R. Sunder. *Det Moderne India's Podcast*, no. 64. Accessed March 28, 2025. https://www.dmi.no

65. Angela Duckworth, *Grit: The Power of Passion and Perseverance* (New York: Scribner, 2016), 8–10.

66. NASA. "Kalpana Chawla Biography." NASA, February 1, 2003. https://www.nasa.gov/sites/default/files/atoms/files/kalpana_chawla.pdf.

67. Bailey, Alyssa. "Amal Clooney's Vanderbilt Graduation Speech Calls for Courage above All." ELLE, May 11, 2018. https://www.elle.com/culture/celebrities/a20660922/amal-clooney-vanderbilt-commencement-speech-on-courage/?

68. New York Road Runners. "Grete Waitz." NYRR Hall of Fame, 2012. https://www.nyrr.org/run/photos-and-stories/hall-of-fame/grete-waitz.

69. "NATIONAL CONFERENCE on 'Dynamics of Women's Movement in India: Historical Legacy and Contemporary Challenges' Supported by ICHR." Accessed March 27, 2025. https://ijmrtjournal.com/wp-content/uploads/2021/07/ichr.pdf.

70. Chattopadhyay S. 2025, Interview by R. Sunder, February 7, 2025 og-administrasjon/det-moderne-india-(e-bok)/p-10024791-no/.

71. Kumari, Shalinee. "Inside a Delhi 'Warrior Mom's' Fight for Clean Air." Eco-Business, March 10, 2025. https://www.eco-business.com/news/inside-a-delhi-warrior-moms-fight-for-clean-air/.

72. NatStrat. "Strategic Dimensions of Polar Studies: An Indian Perspective." https://www.natstrat.org, 2023. https://www.natstrat.org/articledetail/publications/strategic-dimensions-of-polar-studies-an-indian-perspective-54.html.

73. Masten, Ann S. *Ordinary Magic: Resilience in Development.* New York: Guilford Press, 2014.

74. Michael Rutter, "Resilience as a Dynamic Concept," *Development and Psychopathology* 24, no. 2 (2012): 335–344, https://doi.org/10.1017/S0954579412000028

75. Uma Chakravarti, *Rewriting History: The Life and Times of Savitribai Phule* (New Delhi: Zubaan, 2013).

76. "Arundhati Roy: Literature and Activism," *The Guardian*, last modified May 12, 2020, https://www.theguardian.com/books/arundhati-roy.

77. Sofia Falk, "Changing Systems, Not Women," *TEDxStockholm*, 2014.   https://www.ted.com/talks/sofia_falk_changing_systems_not_women

78. Hina Aslam. "Fikk Dalai Lama til Norge for å unngå tvangsekteskap." *Dagsavisen*, April 2, 2022. https://www.dagsavisen.no/fremtiden/nyheter/2022/04/02/fikk-dalai-lama-til-norge-for-a-unnga-tvangsekteskap/.

79. Heysuccess.com. "International Student Festival in Trondheim - ISFiT 2025 - HeySuccess," 2025. https://www.heysuccess.com/opportunity/International-Student-Festival-in-Trondheim-ISFiT25-3744.

80. *Stien Forlag, Nidelvas hemmeligheter* (Trondheim: Stien Forlag, 2023).

81. Bjørby, Inger. "Æresdrap og tvangsekteskap i litteratur for ungdom." In *Den nødvendige samtalen: Barne- og ungdomslitteratur på tvers av grenser*, edited by Elise Seip Tønnessen, 249–264. Oslo: Universitetsforlaget, 2017. https://www.scup.com/doi/10.18261/978-82-15-02955-9-2017-15.

82. LeanIn.Org and McKinsey & Company, *The State of Black Women in Corporate America*, 2020, https://leanin.org/research/state-of-black-women-in-corporate-america.

83. LeanIn.Org and McKinsey & Company, *Women in the Workplace 2021: Women of Color Continue to Have a Worse*

Experience at Work, 2021, https://leanin.org/women-in-the-workplace/2021/women-of-color-continue-to-have-a-worse-experience-at-work.

84. "Kalpana Saroj: The Original Slumdog Millionaire," *BBC News*, last modified February 20, 2013. https://www.bbc.com/news/world-asia-india-21523601

85. Shiva, Vandana. *Staying Alive: Women, Ecology and Development.* London: Zed Books, 1989.

86. Brunner, Nicki. "Stepping into Her Power: Deepa Purushothaman's Journey from Corporate America to Forming New Spaces for Women of Color in the Workplace - QRCA." QRCA, July 11, 2022. https://www.qrcaviews.org/2022/07/11/stepping-into-her-power-deepa-purushothamans-journey-from-corporate-america-to-forming-new-spaces-for-women-of-color-in-the-workplace/.

87. Deepa Purushothaman, *The First, the Few, the Only: How Women of Color Can Redefine Power in Corporate America* (New York: Harper Business, 2022).

88. Li, Jian, Timothy A Matthews, Thomas Clausen, and Reiner Rugulies. "Workplace Discrimination and Risk of Hypertension: Findings from a Prospective Cohort Study in the United States." *Journal of the American Heart Association* 12, no. 9 (April 26, 2023). https://doi.org/10.1161/jaha.122.027374.

89. Deepa Purushothaman, "Being First Need Not Be the Only," *SmartBrief,* April 7, 2022, https://www.smartbrief.com/original/deepa-purushothaman-being-first-need-not-be-the-only.

90. Sudha Murthy, "Appro JRD," *Tata Group*, July 2019, https://www.tata.com/newsroom/heritage/appro-jrd-tata-sudha-murthy-tribute.

91. Gro Harlem Brundtland: Mother of Sustainable Development," *Norway in the UN*, June 14, 2017, https://www.norway.no/en/missions/un/norway-and-the-un/norways-rich-history-at-the-un/important-norwegians-in-un-history/gro/.

92. World Commission on Environment and Development. "Report of the World Commission on Environment and Development: Our Common Future." United Nations, 1987. https://sustainabledevelopment.un.org/content/documents/5987our-common-future.pdf.

93. Ela R. Bhatt, *We Are Poor but So Many: The Story of Self-Employed Women in India* (Oxford: Oxford University Press, 2006).

94. Lise Klaveness, "Calls Out for Change at the FIFA Congress," *Norges Fotballforbund*, March 31, 2022, https://www.fotball.no/tema/nff-nyheter/2022/calls-out-for-change-at-the-fifa-congress/.

95. Norges Fotballforbund. "Calls out for Change at the FIFA Congress." fotball.no - Norges Fotballforbund, 2022. https://www.fotball.no/tema/nff-nyheter/2022/calls-out-for-change-at-the-fifa-congress/.

96. Klaveness L. (2022) *Speeches at the award ceremony for the Freedom of Expression Foundation Tribute to Lise Klaveness.* Fritt Ord available at https://frittord.no/en/news/speeches-at-the-award-ceremony-for-the-freedom-of-expression-foundation-tribute-to-lise-klaveness (accessed 19 Mar. 2025).

97. Isabelle Ringnes, quoted in Martine Aurdal, "Isabelle Ringnes: Den Kvinnelige Teknologigründeren," *Dagbladet Magasinet*, April 15, 2017, https://www.dagbladet.no/magasinet/isabelle-ringnes-den-kvinnelige-teknologigrunderen/67489389.

98. Radha Ramaswami Basu, "From Silicon Valley to Social Impact," *TEDxGateway*, January 2018, https://www.ted.com/talks/radha_basu_from_silicon_valley_to_social_impact

99. Radha Ramaswami Basu, "From Silicon Valley to Social Impact," *TEDxGateway*, January 2018, https://www.ted.com/talks/radha_basu_from_silicon_valley_to_social_impact

100. Berit A. *The Five Master Suppression Techniques*. Kilden available at https://kjonnsforskning.no/nb/five-master-suppression-techniques (accessed 19 Mar. 2025).

101. LVC News. "Gender Equality and Mental Health: Breaking Barriers in the Workplace." Lebanon Valley College, 2023. https://www.lvc.edu/news/gender-equality-and-mental-health-breaking-barriers-in-the-workplace/

102. LVC News. "Gender Equality and Mental Health: Breaking Barriers in the Workplace." Lebanon Valley College, 2023. https://www.lvc.edu/news/gender-equality-and-mental-health-breaking-barriers-in-the-workplace/

103. LVC News. "Gender Equality and Mental Health: Breaking Barriers in the Workplace." Lebanon Valley College, 2023. https://www.lvc.edu/news/gender-equality-and-mental-health-breaking-barriers-in-the-workplace/

104. American Academy of Arts and Sciences. "Women, Power, and Leadership." Dædalus, 2020. https://www.amacad.org/publication/daedalus/women-power-leadership

105. American Academy of Arts and Sciences. "Women, Power, and Leadership." Dædalus, 2020. https://www.amacad.org/publication/daedalus/women-power-leadership

106. American Academy of Arts and Sciences. "Women, Power, and Leadership." Dædalus, 2020. https://www.amacad.org/publication/daedalus/women-power-leadership

107. American Academy of Arts and Sciences. "Women, Power, and Leadership." Dædalus, 2020. https://www.amacad.org/publication/daedalus/women-power-leadership

108. Amanatullah, Emily T., and Catherine H. Tinsley. "Punishing Female Negotiators for Asserting Too Much... or Not Enough: Exploring Why Advocacy Moderates Backlash Against Assertive Female Negotiators." *Organizational Behavior and Human Decision Processes* 120, no. 1 (2013): 110-122.

109. Kark, Ronit, and Alice H. Eagly. "Gender and Leadership: Negotiating the Labyrinth." In *American Psychologist*, 65, no. 3 (2010): 163-171.

110. Heilman, Madeline E., and Michelle C. Haynes. "No Credit Where Credit Is Due: Attributional Rationalization of Women's Success in Male-Female Teams." *Journal of Applied Psychology* 90, no. 5 (2005): 905-916.

111. Ely, Robin J., and Deborah L. Rhode. "Women and Leadership: Defining the Challenges." In *Handbook of Leadership Theory and Practice*, edited by Nitin Nohria and Rakesh Khurana, 377-410. Boston: Harvard Business Press, 2010.

112. Nooyi, Indra. *My Life in Full: Work, Family, and Our Future.* New York: Portfolio, 2021.

113. Sandholt R. K. (2022). *Skarstein choked with tears: - Really tough*. Dagbladet available at https://www.dagbladet.no/sport/gratkvalt-skarstein---skikkelig-toft/75123850 (accessed on 20 Mar. 2025).

114. Hovland, Eirik. "Skårsteins VM-jul: Hyttefeiring Uten Vann og Kloakk." *VG*, December 25, 2023. https://www.vg.no/sport/i/7dyxRw/skarsteins-vm-jul-hyttefeiring-uten-vann-og-kloakk.

115. Basarkod, V. 2025. "Navigating Indian and Nordic Leadership." Interview by R. Sunder. *Det Moderne India's Podcast.* Accessed March 27, 2025. https://www.dmi.no

116. India Briefing. (2024, September 23). *A Promising Future for India-Finland Collaboration*. India Briefing News. https://www.india-briefing.com/news/a-promising-future-for-india-finland-collaboration-34562.html/

117. Ammundsen, Amanda, and Vera Rocha. "Empowering Women in Business." (2024).

118. Andresen, K. 2025. "Women-Led Development." Interview by R. Sunder. *Det Moderne India's Podcast.* Accessed March 27, 2025. https://www.dmi.no

119. Shah, A. 2025. "Ajaita Shah's Vision for a 100-Million-Woman Economy." Interview by R. Sunder. *Det Moderne India's Podcast.*

120. Swati Ganeshan. "Blue Economy: India's Pathway to Sustainable, Secure, and Resilient Economy." ResearchGate. TERI, July 2022. https://www.researchgate.net/publication/362377058_Blue_Economy_India's_Pathway_to_Sustainable_Secure_and_Resilient_Economy.

121. Holte, A. 2025. "Challenges in Recruiting Women in India Podcast Series—Leadership: Paving the Way as the First." Interview by R. Sunder. *Det Moderne India's Podcast*, no. 66. Accessed March 28, 2025. https://www.dmi.no

122. Andresen, K. 2025. "Women-Led Development." Interview by R. Sunder. *Det Moderne India's Podcast.* Accessed March 27, 2025. https://www.dmi.no

123. Shah, A. 2025. "Ajaita Shah's Vision for a 100-Million-Woman Economy." Interview by R. Sunder. Delhi, February 14.

124. Frontier Markets. "Partnerships | Frontier Markets," 2016. https://www.frontiermkts.com/partnerships.

125. Frontier Markets. "Our Impact | Frontier Markets," 2016. https://www.frontiermkts.com/our-impact.

126. Jejeebhoy, Shireen. "ENDING CHILD MARRIAGE in INDIA Drivers and Strategies," 2019. https://www.unicef.org/india/media/2556/file/Drivers-strategies-for-ending-child-marriage.pdf.

127. Sunder, Rina. "Det Moderne India (E-Bok)." Gyldendal. no, 2019. https://www.gyldendal.no/faglitteratur/e-boeker/oekonomi-og-administrasjon/det-moderne-india-(e-bok)/p-10024791-no/.

128. "Patriarchal Moments." Accessed March 27, 2025. https://library.oapen.org/bitstream/handle/20.500.12657/58787/9781474237987.pdf?sequence=1&isAllowed=y.

129. Taulia. "Norway Payment Terms Regulations | Taulia," June 10, 2024. https://taulia.com/payment-terms/norway/.

130. Basarkod, V. 2025. "Navigating Indian and Nordic Leadership." Interview by R. Sunder. *Det Moderne India's Podcast.* Accessed March 27, 2025. https://www.dmi.no

131. Gharahkhani, M. 2023. "Men Who Support Women." Interview by R. Sunder. *Det Moderne India's Podcast.* Accessed March 27, 2025. https://www.dmi.no

132. Ringnes, C. 2023. "Men Who Support Women." Interview by R. Sunder. *Det Moderne India's Podcast.* Accessed March 28, 2025. https://www.detmoderneindia.no

133. Ringnes, C., Lund, C., Soin, R., and Finnes, S. 2022. "Men Who Support Women." Interview by R. Sunder. *Det Moderne India's Podcast*, no. 32. Accessed March 28, 2025. https://www.detmoderneindia.no

134. Basarkod, V. 2025. "Navigating Indian and Nordic Leadership." Interview by R. Sunder. *Det Moderne India's Podcast*, no. 70. Accessed March 28, 2025. https://www.dmi.no

135. NASSCOM and Zinnov, *India's Tech Industry: Women in the Workforce*, 2022, https://nasscom.in.

136. Oda Network. *Tech-Norge 2023: Kvinner i IT.* https://odanettverk.no.

137. Invest India, "Women Entrepreneurship Platform (WEP)," https://www.investindia.gov.in/team-india-blogs/women-entrepreneurship-platform-wep.

138. Government of India, Ministry of Electronics & IT, *Digital India Initiatives*, https://www.meity.gov.in.

139. Infosys. "Diversity and Inclusion." Accessed March 23, 2025. https://www.infosys.com/about/diversity-inclusion.html.

140. Infosys, *Environmental, Social and Governance Report 2023*, https://www.infosys.com.

141. UNESCO, *Cracking the Code: Girls' and Women's Education in STEM*, 2017, https://unesdoc.unesco.org/ark:/48223/pf0000253479.

142. McKinsey & Company, "Women in the Workplace 2022," https://www.mckinsey.com.

143. McKinsey & Company. "Women in the Workplace 2022." October 2022. https://www.mckinsey.com.

144. Girl Tech Fest Norway, "About," https://girltechfest.no; She Economy, "Vision," https://sheconomy.no.

145. Mali Hole Skogen, interview by Rina Sunder, Delhi, February, 2025

146. <?>Women in Tech Sweden. "About Us." Accessed March 23, 2025. https://www.womenintech.se/about-us/

147. UN Women. "Generation Equality Forum: Technology and Innovation Coalition Launches Action Plan." July 2, 2021. https://www.unwomen.org/en/news/stories/2021/7/feature-generation-equality-forum-technology-and-innovation-coalition-launches-action-plan

148. European Commission. "Women to the Top (W2T)." *Projects Database*, 2005. https://ec.europa.eu/employment_social/emplweb/gender-equality/projects (or alternative if this page no longer exists—if needed, I can find an archived version)

149. Mayank Saxena (CEO of CodingPro), interview by Rina Sunder, Delhi, February, 2025

150. Tietoevry. "The Nordic Paradox in Tech – Women Believe in the Power of Technology but Still Shy Away from It." March 6, 2023. https://www.tietoevry.com/en/newsroom/news/2023/3/the-nordic-paradox-in-tech--women-believe-in-the-power-of-technology--but-still-shy-away-from-it/

151. Tietoevry. "The Nordic Paradox in Tech – Women Believe in the Power of Technology but Still Shy Away from It." March 6, 2023. https://www.tietoevry.com/en/newsroom/news/2023/3/the-nordic-paradox-in-tech--women-believe-in-the-power-of-technology--but-still-shy-away-from-it/

152. Tietoevry. "The Nordic Paradox in Tech – Women Believe in the Power of Technology but Still Shy Away from It." March 6, 2023. https://www.tietoevry.com/en/newsroom/news/2023/3/the-nordic-paradox-in-tech--women-believe-in-the-power-of-technology--but-still-shy-away-from-it/

153. OECD. *Parental Leave Systems and the Division of Parental Responsibilities in the Nordic Countries*. Paris: OECD Publishing, 2021. https://www.oecd.org.

154. OECD. *Bridging the Digital Gender Divide: Include, Upskill, Innovate*. Paris: OECD Publishing, 2018. https://www.oecd.org/sti/bridging-the-digital-gender-divide.pdf.

155. OECD. *Bridging the Digital Gender Divide: Include, Upskill, Innovate*. Paris: OECD Publishing, 2018. https://www.oecd.org/sti/bridging-the-digital-gender-divide.pdf.

156. Tietoevry. "The Nordic Paradox in Tech – Women Believe in the Power of Technology but Still Shy Away from It." March 6, 2023. https://www.tietoevry.com/en/newsroom/news/2023/3/the-nordic-paradox-in-tech--women-believe-in-the-power-of-technology--but-still-shy-away-from-it/

157. ICT Norway. "Innspill til NFD: Slik får vi flere kvinner i teknologibransjen." November 21, 2022. https://www.ict-norway.no/aktuelt/innspill-til-nfd-slik-far-vi-flere-kvinner-i-teknologibransjen/

158. Invest India. "Women Entrepreneurship Platform (WEP)." Accessed March 23, 2025. https://www.investindia.gov.in/team-india-blogs/women-entrepreneurship-platform-wep.

159. UN Women. "India Passes Law to Protect Women against Workplace Harassment." February 2020. https://www.unwomen.org/en/news/stories/2020/2/news-new-law-to-protect-women-against-workplace-harassment-india.

160. Mohanty, S. 2025. "India's IT Gender Balance: A Model for the Nordics Podcast Series— Cracking the Code: How India is Leading in Gender Diversity in Tech " Interview by R. Sunder. *Det Moderne India's Podcast*, no.69https://open.spotify.com/episode/41MNSY0nBmgfOIyrySJF1b, Accessed March 28, 2025.

161. Pib.gov.in. "PARLIAMENT QUESTION: GOVERNMENT SCHEMES to PROMOTE SCIENCE EDUCATION among GIRLS," 2025. https://pib.gov.in/PressReleaseIframePage.aspx?PRID=2113279

162. Singh, Shalini. "Empowering Women in STEM: India's WISE-KIRAN Initiative." Observer Voice, February 7, 2025. https://observervoice.com/empowering-women-in-stem-indias-wise-kiran-initiative-94711/.

163. dst.gov.in. "CURIE Initiative of DST Enhancing Research Facilities in Women Universities | Department of Science & Technology," n.d. https://dst.gov.in/pressrelease/curie-initiative-dst-enhancing-research-facilities-women-universities.

164. Cherian, S. 2025. "India's IT Gender Balance: A Model for the Nordics Podcast Series—Lighthouse Leadership: How Wipro Sets the Standard for DEIB in Tech." Interview by R. Sunder. *Det Moderne India's Podcast*, no. 68. Accessed March 28, 2025. https://www.dmi.no

165. Cherian, S. 2025. "Lighthouse Leadership: How Wipro Sets the Standard for DEIB in Tech." Interview by R. Sunder. *Det Moderne India's Podcast*. Accessed March 27, 2025. https://www.dmi.no

166. Mali Hole Skogen, interview by Rina Sunder, Delhi, February, 2025. Accessed March 28, 2025.